Canadian Political Structure and Public Administration

A Law Enforcement Perspective

Geoffrey J. Booth & Dennis M. Roughley

2001

EMOND MONTGOMERY PUBLICATIONS LIMITED

TORONTO, CANADA

Printed in Canada.

Edited, designed, and typeset by WordsWorth Communications, Toronto.
Cover design by Susan Darrach, Darrach Design.

We acknowledge the financial support of the Government of Canada through the Book Publishing Industry Development Program (BPIDP) for our publishing activities.

Canadian Cataloguing in Publication Data

Booth, Geoffrey J., 1962–
Canadian political structure and public administration: a law enforcement perspective

ISBN 1-55239-053-5

1. Canada — Politics and government.   I. Roughley, Dennis M., 1941–   . II. Title.

JL75.B66 2000   320.471   C00-932906-4

For our students

We would also like to acknowledge David Brown, Drew Dunning, and Tanya Kienapple for their contributions to this project. Special thanks as well to Marian Harris for her support and encouragement throughout the process.

Contents

■ *Part* III   **PUBLIC ADMINISTRATION   89**

APPENDIX A   THE CANADIAN CHARTER OF RIGHTS AND FREEDOMS   193

GLOSSARY OF TERMS   199

Preface

Our purpose for writing this text is twofold. First, we hope to help students make a theoretical and practical connection among the realms of Canadian political structure, public administration, and law enforcement. We believe that students need to clearly understand the importance of democratic processes and how each process interacts with and affects individuals' role in law enforcement. One of the major challenges of teaching these subjects has been to demonstrate how the political process affects individuals in their personal and professional environments. No introductory-level texts in political science address this concern, and hence present both students and instructors with the challenge of making what is learned both relevant and applicable. Our goal, therefore, has been to overcome this obstacle by placing politics and public administration in the context of justice, public safety, and law enforcement.

Second, we recognize the increasing expectation of citizens and governing bodies to ensure that candidates seeking a career in public law enforcement understand the nature of government and its operation with reference to the Canadian criminal justice system, as well as understand their responsibilities within this elaborate system. In an era of high professional standards and a growing desire for public accountability, it is vital that students have a firm grasp of this knowledge as they enter the workplace.

In this text, we have incorporated our many years of collective experience in politics, policing, research, and education to produce current material that we know will prove to be both informative and useful to students and their instructors. Enjoy!

Geoffrey J. Booth and Dennis M. Roughley
December 2000

PART I

Introduction to Politics and Public Administration

CHAPTER 1

Introductory Concepts

CHAPTER OBJECTIVES

After completing this chapter, you should be able to:

◆ Define politics and the various ways in which it affects Canadian citizens.

◆ Explain the evolution of government as a social institution and how we as citizens determine the extent of a government's authority and legitimacy.

◆ Describe the relationship between politics and public administration from a practical, as well as a theoretical, standpoint.

◆ Understand, in general, the purpose and content of this text.

WHAT IS POLITICS?

To many of us, the terms "politics" and "public administration" are both mysterious and intimidating. This discomfort is reinforced daily by media reports of dishonesty, corruption, and ineptitude, which seem to pop up at regular intervals. It may surprise you that anyone pays attention to what goes on in government, let alone becomes involved in public life. However, thousands of people continue to play a part in governing this country, and without them we would in fact have no country. The system of government we live with today reveals much about our history and our values as Canadians. And, despite the seemingly endless barrage of criticism hurled at it, Canada's government remains one of the best models of problem solving through political compromise and dialogue in the world today.

How did we earn such an enviable global reputation? What are the essential components of Canadian political structure, and how do they interact with one another? What is the historical context for this intricate and ever-changing dance among political partners? And finally, how does all of this express itself in the realms of law enforcement and public safety? These are but a few of the many topics we will cover in the chapters that follow. To begin, we should define some terms necessary for a clear understanding of politics and public administration in Canada.

At its root, **politics** is fundamentally about power and who decides how this power is to be used. We can think of power as the capacity of

politics
the social system that decides who has power and how it is to be used in governing the society's affairs

3

one person or group to impose decisions on another person or group. In other words, politics is about getting your own way.

There are many ways to get your own way—using influence, persuasion, brute force, charisma, negotiation, or compromise are only some of them. Perhaps without knowing it, you have already experienced examples of this in your own life. Growing up, you may have had to share a television with other members of your family. How did you decide who got to watch what program at what time of day? What if something you wanted to watch was in someone else's time slot? What about programs that exceeded your time allotment? Did your age, attitude, or status have any influence on whether you got to watch what you wanted? What role did your parents play in determining what was acceptable viewing for your family? All of these questions help to illustrate the power relations between you and members of your family. Now consider what it would be like to come to a decision about virtually anything in a country of 30 million people. This happens every day as government officials engage in the shared task of keeping Canada running. We elect politicians at the federal, provincial, and municipal levels of government to represent our individual and collective interests and bring them to the attention of the state.

WHAT IS GOVERNMENT?

government
a formal system within which political power is exercised

At first glance, the answer to the question "What is government?" seems obvious, yet a simple response is elusive. **Government** is a formal system within which political power is exercised. Still, this doesn't capture the incredible complexity of government, both as a concept and as a practice. Government is present in so many aspects of our lives that many of its activities go unnoticed.

Government has a long history dating back as far as the beginnings of human civilization itself, and many people have written about its form and function. Basically, in a modern, democratic society such as Canada's, government exists because it embraces two fundamental political concepts: authority and legitimacy. Both are closely related, and both have important implications for law enforcement. **Authority** refers to government's ability to make decisions that are binding on its citizens. As long as the general population accepts that some groups or individuals in society have power to issue and enforce these commands, they will obey them. If citizens respect where the decisions come from, they will accept them, whether they agree with these decisions or not. **Legitimacy** refers to the moral obligation citizens feel to obey the laws and pronouncements issued by those in authority.

authority
government's ability to make decisions that are binding on its citizens

legitimacy
the moral obligation citizens feel to obey the laws and pronouncements issued by those in authority

Taken together, these concepts explain why we as Canadians abide by the laws our governments make for us. Even if we think that a law is misguided or misses the point, we still recognize that our politicians have the right to pass laws for the greater good of society. If each Canadian decided instead to disobey laws whenever he or she chose, the system of law and its enforcement would simply break down. Imagine the implications this scenario could have in the area of transportation. The absence of a general acceptance of rules, enforced by police and other authorities, would quickly lead to misunderstandings over road use, disputes arising from accidents, arbitrary speed limits, and ultimately unsafe conditions for everyone. As members of a society that recognizes the wisdom of authority and legitimacy in its political system, we assume that our governments will act for the greater good of society, even if this means that our personal freedom is limited by these decisions.

In a democracy, the concepts of authority and legitimacy are tied directly to what is known as the **rule of law**. The rule of law ensures that all citizens, regardless of social rank, are subject to the laws, courts, and other legal institutions of the nation. For instance, a prime minister who is found guilty of a crime cannot pass a law to make his or her infraction legitimate. The rule of law also demands that *all* government actions be legal—that is, they must be approved and accepted by a justice system that is free from state interference. This guards against the possibility that government officials might resort to illegal actions to accomplish a task. This is also why police forces take such care to ensure that officers respect the law in the course of carrying out their duties. Violating an accused's rights or collecting evidence illegally may damage the credibility of an investigation, resulting in charges being dropped and/or legal action being taken by the defendant. The rule of law ensures fair and equitable treatment by a government, and as we will see later, it forms an integral part of Canada's system of justice and public safety.

rule of law
the concept that all citizens, regardless of social rank, are subject to the laws, courts, and other legal institutions of the nation

How Law Enforcement Fits In

Policing is an integral part of Canada's public justice system and is therefore one link responsible for preserving the rule of law and functioning within its parameters. If people lose faith in their government, there is a danger that they will also lose faith in the rule of law. This is why as a society we go to such lengths not only to "do justice"—ensure the rights of accused individuals, make sure that police follow proper legal procedures, and so on—but also to demonstrate to all Canadians that justice is seen to be done.

How and Why We Accept the Rule of Law

The process of demonstrating that justice is seen to be done belongs in large part to the media, which cover both the successes and the failures of the justice system in this regard. The public's right to know the details of a court case, for example, is common practice. In some rare situations, however, this right is suspended in order to ensure an accused person's right to a fair trial. Public trust in the legal system can never be taken for granted in any society. We must be reminded through the words and deeds of public officials that every effort is being made to ensure that justice is done so that when problems occur they can be remedied efficiently and effectively.

An important reason Canadians live within the framework of laws, regulations, and political decisions is because they can hold their political representatives accountable through the process of elections. Elections are a way to ensure continued citizen support for the authority and legitimacy of their governments, and they force elected politicians to be accountable for what they have done (or not done) during their term as elected representatives. As we will see in later chapters, Canadian political tradition, the process of choosing candidates, party affiliation, and other socioeconomic issues play a large part in determining how the public's judgment plays itself out in the political scene.

THE ART OF GOVERNMENT: POLITICS AND PUBLIC ADMINISTRATION

The aim of this textbook is to give you a practical overview of Canada's political structure and the bureaucracy through which much of its operation is carried out. Politics and public administration, although sharing a common purpose of furthering the public good, often go about doing so in different ways. The nature of this relationship, as we will see, can be complementary or competitive, resulting in new approaches to government policy.

For the purposes of this text, the term "politics" will be used to refer to the work of politicians at the federal, provincial, and municipal levels of government who are elected by the people they represent. We treat the subject of politics separately from that of public administration because, although one can argue that all aspects of government involve both political and administrative elements, it is politicians who must ultimately answer to us for what their particular level of government has done from one election to the next.

public administration
the branch of the political structure, consisting of public employees, that turns the policy decisions of elected politicians into action

civil service
people who are directly tied to the administrative function of a particular level of government

public service
the civil service

Public administration is more challenging to define because, as we will discover later in this text, it can be understood to include every non-elected person who is employed by government. Often referred to as the **civil service** or **public service**, this branch of Canadian political structure hypothetically includes anyone employed in a publicly funded activity, such as policing, firefighting, and teaching. However, convention normally limits public administration to people who are directly tied to the administrative function of a particular level of government, such as policy implementation and evaluation. The public service takes the policy decisions of elected politicians and turns them into concrete action. For example, suppose a local municipality's councillors hear concerns from constituents about the need for a sidewalk to help children travel safely to and from a school in an area with heavy traffic. The political will of the council is dictated to the municipality's public works department, which in turn sends out a crew to construct the sidewalk.

This simple example skips many of the intermediary steps involved in accomplishing such a task, but it illustrates what might be called the "classic" model of communication between politicians and public servants.

As we will see in later chapters, a complex system of communication exists among these branches of Canadian political structure, and this system often blurs the line between those responsible for creating policy and those who are ultimately held responsible for implementing it.

WHY STUDY POLITICAL STRUCTURE AND PUBLIC ADMINISTRATION?

You should now have some idea as to why students interested in the fields of justice and public safety should understand Canadian political structure and public administration. As an agent of law enforcement, it is essential that you understand your legal rights and obligations. This knowledge extends beyond the rules and regulations of your employer to encompass where and how the legitimate authority of the state is delegated to public agencies, such as police forces, whose sworn duty it is to uphold laws passed by the state and to maintain respect for the rule of law. In this sense, you represent the public good and therefore have a responsibility to know how government works—that is, the origin and implementation of public policy through government legislation. This knowledge enables you to understand and appreciate more fully your role in the overall administration of justice and to understand the roles of other key players in developing, interpreting, and administering law.

This text, and the course it represents, also provides you with an understanding of your rights and responsibilities as a Canadian citizen. This too should help to better acquaint you with the structure and day-to-day practice of government at the federal, provincial, and municipal levels and with their relationship to justice and public safety. Your familiarity with Canadian political structure and public administration will give you an advantage as you prepare to meet the challenges and changes currently facing law enforcement in Canada.

STRUCTURE OF THIS BOOK

Following is a brief overview of some of the topics you will encounter as you read through the sections of this book. Keep in mind that while each chapter attempts to focus on a particular area of interest, all of the topics are interrelated because issues and decisions in one sector of government and public administration often have an impact on other sectors.

Chapter 2 presents a brief history of the events that led to Confederation in 1867 and how Canada's political structure was established at that time. The chapter explains the origin of the three levels of government in the context of the Canadian constitution, and provides some historical background that will help you better understand the political issues that face Canadians today.

Chapter 3 focuses on the constitution from its inception as the *British North America Act* through its patriation in 1982, including attempts at constitutional reform. Attention is given to the *Charter of Rights and Freedoms*[1] and its impact on Canadians' individual and collective rights, as well as to its effects on law enforcement and the role of the courts in the political and constitutional process.

Chapter 4 begins with an explanation of representative and responsible government, and then explores the electoral process and the role of candidates. It goes on to examine the structure and roles of the three levels of government—federal, provincial, and municipal—and defines their executive, legislative, and judicial functions. The process of making laws at each level of government is also explained. The chapter introduces the interrelationships among the three levels of government, a topic that will be explored in more detail in later chapters. Chapter 4 also introduces First Nations in the Canadian political structure, presenting a brief history of the relationship between First Nations and non-Native government.

Chapter 5 describes the evolution of government services in Canada in general and law enforcement in particular. The chapter then encourages you to look at the "big picture" by using what you learned in the previous five chapters to discuss some current issues in Canadian politics as they relate to policing and the justice system. Particular attention is paid to influences on the political process at all levels of government and how these have direct and indirect effects on law enforcement. Chapter 5 concludes with a discussion of police responses to changing social realities.

With this political context in place, the focus shifts to an emphasis on public administration. Chapters 6 and 7 explore the meaning of public administration with a view to helping you recognize its relevance and relation to the political process. In particular, you will discover how politics and public administration entities rely on each other for mutual benefit and, ultimately, survival. It will become evident that tension also characterizes this relationship as political and administrative forces attempt to achieve specific goals. These chapters also briefly summarize theories of bureaucracy to see how these have influenced the evolution of a modern public service in Canada. You will then have an opportunity to explore the similarities and differences between private and public administration, giving particular attention to recent trends toward government privatization of public facilities, such as prisons.

Chapter 8 focuses on the "glue" that binds politics and administration—public policy. Using examples, the chapter illustrates the many complex—and often unpredictable—stages that take place while policy is being created, implemented, and evaluated. The chapter ends by examining the influence of outside forces in the policy process by analyzing recent political activism within police unions, in particular the Toronto Police Association. By examining union initiatives such as Operation True Blue, we will consider what can happen when decision-making authority is challenged or threatened.

Chapters 9 and 10 complete our exploration of the complex world of public administration by examining the structure and organization of the civil service in Canada today, with particular emphasis on those components that play a role in the system of justice and law enforcement. These chapters describe the many ministries, agencies, and Crown corporations that constitute the public service. You will discover how public policy is transformed into administrative law and become aware of the differences between this type of legislation and others, such as constitutional law. As well, you will see how politicians and public servants work together to meet the challenges that arise in government. By analyzing examples, such as the role of Ontario's Special Investigations Unit (SIU) in overseeing police activity, you will also discover that disagreement and conflict are an ongoing part of the relationship between government and the public service.

Chapter 11 focuses on your part as a constituent in our government system. The chapter presents some of the benefits of getting involved in politics, especially at the municipal level, as well as some suggestions on how to do so. As you prepare for a career in law enforcement, it is our hope that at this point you will understand and feel confident about your role in Canadian society, both as a representative of law enforcement and as a private citizen.

SUMMARY

Politics, public administration, and government are different, but interrelated, components of the Canadian political structure. Politics is about power and who decides how it is to be used in the management of a country's affairs. Government is a system of organizing a society so that disputes can be resolved or prevented. Public administration, as the term is used in this book, refers to the process of administering the functions of government as well as to the people who perform those functions (often called the civil service).

How a society chooses to structure these components can tell us much about the values of that society. For instance, Canada's political structure is a federation that divides jurisdiction over major policy areas between the federal and provincial governments. This structure is rooted in our constitution, but the federal government's traditional role—a role that has been allotted most of the political power—is being increasingly challenged by the provinces. Canada also faces the challenges and opportunities of being a multicultural society and a nation of regions with different socioeconomic realities.

The concepts of authority and legitimacy, which are closely linked to the rule of law, help to explain why Canadians are willing to allow governments and their representatives to make laws and policy decisions and are willing to abide by those laws and decisions.

The remainder of this book will discuss these topics and the interrelationships among them in more detail, with a view to placing the role of law enforcement in a larger political context.

KEY TERMS

politics	rule of law
government	public administration
authority	civil service
legitimacy	public service

NOTES

1. *Canadian Charter of Rights and Freedoms*, part I of the *Constitution Act, 1982*, RSC 1985, app. 2, no. 44.

EXERCISES

■ MULTIPLE CHOICE

1. The rule of law ensures that
   a. all citizens are subject to the laws of the nation
   b. even top-ranking politicians cannot override the law
   c. government treats all citizens fairly and equitably
   d. all government actions are legal
   e. all of the above

2. While politics is about managing public affairs, government is about
   a. the moral obligation citizens feel to obey laws
   b. organizing people to prevent conflict
   c. policing people
   d. electing representatives who do what we say
   e. who has power and how this power is used

3. Authority refers to
   a. the right of law enforcement agents to detain people
   b. the obligation citizens feel to obey those in authority
   c. government's ability to make decisions that are binding on its citizens
   d. the dominance of a particular government body's decisions
   e. the requirement that everyone is subject to the law

4. Government exists because it recognizes two fundamental political principles:

    a. politics and the rule of law

    b. legitimacy and public administration

    c. the rule of law and authority

    d. authority and legitimacy

    e. authority and law enforcement

5. The fundamental role of public administration is to

    a. formulate public policy

    b. make laws for Canadians

    c. govern Canadian society

    d. make decisions that are binding on citizens

    e. turn policy decisions of politicians into concrete action

■ TRUE OR FALSE?

_____ 1. Government has existed for as long as human civilization.

_____ 2. Government's ability to make decisions for citizens is called legitimacy.

_____ 3. Legitimacy is a legal obligation citizens feel to obey the laws of a country.

_____ 4. We make sure the rights of accused individuals are respected and proper legal procedures are followed partly to ensure that citizens do not lose faith in the rule of law.

_____ 5. The prime minister has the right to pass a law to avoid being charged with a crime he or she has committed.

■ SHORT ANSWER

1. Define politics and explain the various ways in which it affects Canadian citizens.

2. How do we as citizens determine the extent of a government's authority and legitimacy?

3. What is the relationship between politics and public administration from a practical, as well as a theoretical, standpoint?

PART II
Political Structure

CHAPTER 2

Unity Through Diversity: Canada Becomes a Nation

CHAPTER OBJECTIVES

After completing this chapter, you should be able to:

◆ Understand the historical development of Canada's federalist system of government.

◆ Explain the British and Canadian roots of Canada's original constitution.

◆ Identify the origins of the three levels of government in Canada.

◆ Describe the division of powers between the federal and provincial governments.

INTRODUCTION

Understanding Canadian politics requires understanding Canadian history. This chapter briefly summarizes some of the major events and factors that have contributed to the current shape and character of our country.

Canada became a country on July 1, 1867. The British North American and British officials who laid its foundations, however, might have some difficulty recognizing it today. This country has undergone many changes over the last one and a half centuries, changes that have had a profound impact on the way Canadians understand themselves and their country.

ROOTS OF CONFEDERATION

Before **Confederation** on July 1, 1867, British North America consisted of a number of scattered, independent colonies, each with its own social, economic, and political history:

◆ British Columbia;

◆ the North-West Territories;

◆ Rupert's Land (a vast area that covered much of the present-day Prairie provinces and northern Ontario and Quebec), which was owned by the Hudson's Bay Company;

Confederation
the union of former British colonies that resulted in the formation of Canada on July 1, 1867

15

- ◆ Upper Canada or Canada West (now Ontario);

- ◆ Lower Canada or Canada East (now Quebec);

- ◆ New Brunswick;

- ◆ Nova Scotia;

- ◆ Prince Edward Island; and

- ◆ Newfoundland.

Earlier attempts at political union had failed. However, by the 1860s, a number of factors coaxed four of the colonies—Canada West, Canada East, New Brunswick, and Nova Scotia—into considering the creation of one central government while retaining their respective rights to govern themselves.

Canada has always been a nation of immigrants. The aboriginal peoples who first lived here came across the land bridge that once connected Asia to North America. Subsequent waves of French and British settlers, and later people from around the world, resulted in a country of ethnic and cultural diversity. However, the populations of the British North American colonies in the 1860s were still small and rural. They were also largely isolated from one another by geography, the sheer size of the land they occupied, and a limited transportation system.

The four founding members of Confederation had little in common. Canada West, the largest colony, had a population mainly made up of English, Scottish, and Irish immigrants. French-speaking Canada East's population was mainly native-born with a shared history going back to the 1600s; the Catholic Church had a strong influence in this colony, where local governments reflected the local church parishes. The much smaller populations of the Atlantic colonies were also mainly native-born and English-speaking.[1]

A proposed political union of the British North American colonies in 1841 failed to resolve many of the political problems that had led to rebellions in 1837 and 1838 in Upper Canada and Lower Canada. The reasons for these rebellions had been building for years, and were the result of class tensions, ethnic tensions in Lower Canada between Francophones and Anglophones, and frustration over the lack of democratic representation in the colonial governments, which were dominated by members of a wealthy elite. In 1840 Britain had united Upper and Lower Canada into the Province of Canada, giving each—now called Canada West and Canada East—equal political representation in a United Assembly, despite the fact that Canada West had a substantially larger population. The new assembly passed laws for both colonies, but its members reflected the interests of their respective territories, reproducing the split between French and English Canadians. Thus the government remained deadlocked. Another form of government was sought, and by the early 1860s, calls to unite the British North American colonies began to take shape. The Atlantic colonies sought a Maritime federation as well to strengthen their economies.

The Desire for Union

A factor that contributed to interest in a new union was the growing desire to build an intercolonial railway to connect all of British North America. The railway would facilitate trade and help bring more settlers into the region. At the time, most transportation was by water. Canals helped to connect the many lakes and rivers to otherwise landlocked areas, but they were of little use in the winter. Railways were a logical alternative. The only problem was their cost—building and maintaining them was extremely expensive, a fact that put railways out of the reach of any one colony. Working together, however, such a venture was feasible.

Confederation also promised trade advantages. Until 1849 the colonies had enjoyed preferential treatment in their trade with Britain. Colonial exports were guaranteed a share of the British market, even if these goods could be obtained more cheaply elsewhere. Britain abandoned this policy after 1849, however, opting for free trade—an economic system based on buying goods at the lowest possible price. The British North American colonies now had to compete among themselves and with bigger, established American competitors who benefited from a much larger population base. It made economic sense for the colonies to unite to create a strong market capable of competing in trade.

Finally, concerns about defence made Confederation seem like a good idea. Since the American Revolution of 1776, the British North American colonies had repeatedly been targets of attack from the Americans. Border invasions during the American Revolution and the War of 1812, in which the United States aimed to seize the colonies, as well as minor incursions during the 1830s, had made the British North Americans distrust the Americans. The time seemed right to band together in the interest of self-preservation.

CONFEDERATION

In September 1864, representatives of the Atlantic colonies—New Brunswick, Nova Scotia, and Prince Edward Island—were meeting in Charlottetown to discuss the possibility of a Maritime union. Representatives from the Province of Canada joined the Charlottetown Conference to try to persuade the Atlantic colonies of the benefits of a larger union. The Atlantic delegates weren't convinced, but agreed to meet with the Canada West and Canada East representatives in Quebec in October to discuss the idea further.

Debates over Confederation and the form of government of the new union continued at the Quebec Conference and in the colonies. Newfoundland took part in these negotiations, as did Prince Edward Island, but these two colonies eventually decided against joining the new union.

Finally, on July 1, 1867, the Dominion of Canada, under Prime Minister John A. Macdonald, was born out of four former colonies when the British Parliament passed the *British North America Act*.[2] Canada's form of government was unique in the world, since our country was part of the

British Commonwealth, its head of state was the British monarch, and its constitution—embodied in the BNA Act—was a British statute. Today Canada is an independent nation, but the decisions made at Confederation continue to affect Canadian government and politics.

The New Government

Canada was born out of a compromise among its four founding provinces. Because of the strong local traditions and allegiances that existed at the time of this political union, the would-be provinces of the new country were reluctant to transfer all of their political power to the newly formed national government. What resulted was a **federal system** whereby political powers were split between a strong central, or federal, government and the governments of the original four provinces. Each level of government was granted certain powers over specific areas, as stated in the BNA Act. Although the federal government was allotted most of the political power, the later growth in importance of areas of provincial jurisdiction, such as health and education, increasingly challenged the position of the federal government to decide many political matters.

federal system
Canada's government structure, which divides political power between the federal government and the provincial governments, with greater power resting in the federal government

A country as geographically vast and culturally diverse as Canada needed a system of government based on equality in a context of diversity. The federal system means that political power is shared between the federal government based in Ottawa and the provincial governments. It is doubtful that Canada would or could have been created in any other way. Today, the federal government serves all Canadians, including the 10 provinces and 3 territories, while each provincial government serves only the people living within that province (the territories, although they have more independence today than in the past, are still financially dependent on the federal government and do not have the same constitutional powers as the provinces).

Confederation was seen by its supporters as a solution for many of the difficulties discussed earlier. It was thought that a union would brace the scattered provinces against possible US aggression and make it easier to defend their navigational rights on the St. Lawrence River and their fishing rights at sea. Confederation was further designed to foster a national economy in which there would be improved transportation facilities, including winter access to the sea. It was hoped that the resources and industries of the provinces would complement one another, thus increasing the prosperity and self-sufficiency of the whole. The Fathers of Confederation also looked toward the future, when the united country would help to speed up the development and settlement of the Canadian northwest and ultimately include a Pacific province.

There was significant pressure for political union, but also equally strong counterpressures calling for local cultures, traditions, and interests to be preserved. These counterpressures were particularly strong in French-speaking Canada and the Maritimes. While a compromise on a federal system was worked out and embodied in the BNA Act, the actual terms of the Act were not universally supported by all the people who were affected, including First Nations, who were placed under the control of the federal government. This helps to explain the continuing struggle to this day for aboriginal recognition and right of self-determination, which will be discussed in later chapters of this book.

POST-CONFEDERATION

Nonetheless, after much debate, political manoeuvring, and rebellions by groups opposed to being part of the union, by 1873 Canada stretched from coast to coast and now also included the Northwest Territories, British Columbia, and Manitoba (which joined Canada in 1870), and Prince Edward Island (which joined in 1873). In 1905 much of the Northwest Territories was split off to become the Yukon Territory, Alberta, and Saskatchewan. Finally, in 1949, Newfoundland became the tenth province. Canada has not stopped evolving as a country, as illustrated by the division of the Northwest Territories yet again to form Nunavut Territory, part of a major settlement of Inuit land claims that came into being on April 1, 1999.[3]

THE CONSTITUTION

British Roots

As mentioned above, the BNA Act was the piece of British legislation that united the four founding provinces of the new country and gave Canada its **constitution**—a document that outlines the basic principles of government of a country and the fundamental rights and freedoms enjoyed by its citizens. The Act also allowed for future provinces to join the federation.

Both the written and the implied parts of the Act bore the unmistakable imprint of Britain, although the federal structure was an important exception. Formally, the Act provided that the British monarch (whose representative in Canada is the governor general) was to be the chief executive officer and head of the new country. There was also to be a **bicameral legislature**—two Houses of Parliament—consisting of the House of Commons and the Senate (explained in more detail in chapter 4), which correspond to the British House of Commons and House of Lords. Each House was to have an equal voice in Canadian legislation, except that, as in the British Parliament, financial measures were to be initiated in the House of Commons. This practice still exists today—no government financial bills may initiate in the Senate. Canada also inherited from Britain

◆ the political party system;

◆ the principle under which executive authority resides in the prime minister and Cabinet and only nominally in the Queen and governor general (which will be discussed in more detail in chapter 4);

constitution
a document that outlines the basic principles of government of a country and the fundamental rights and freedoms enjoyed by its citizens

bicameral legislature
a government structure that consists of two Houses of Parliament; in Canada, the House of Commons and the Senate

- ◆ the principle of responsible government (also discussed in chapter 4), which was hard won by the provinces to Confederation, requiring that the executive must at all times be responsible to and retain the support of a majority of the popularly elected House of Commons; and

- ◆ the theory of the supremacy of Parliament and of the provincial legislatures, within their respective powers, as determined ultimately by the courts.

Canadian Contributions

In addition to those parts of the constitution inherited from British tradition, a large number of conventions and practices of constitutional significance have gradually been developed and established within Canada.

An outstanding exception to the general rule of British influence on the Canadian constitution was Canada's departure from the unitary state. The United Kingdom, then as now, was a unitary state in which the local authorities were established and governed by legislation passed by the British Parliament. At first, in the pre-Confederation conferences, the representatives of what was to become Ontario favoured the creation of a **legislative union**, as the unitary state was then usually called, with power concentrated entirely in the central Parliament and government. It became clear, however, that the French-speaking and Maritime colonies would not agree to surrender complete legislative jurisdiction to any central authority, and that a federal system that gave the provinces the right to make and administer laws relating to mainly local matters was the only practical solution.

legislative union
a structure of government in which power is concentrated in a central Parliament

Division of Powers

The strong regional differences that led each province to insist on retaining certain powers and responsibilities resulted in the **division of powers** between the federal and provincial governments. The powers and responsibilities—or **jurisdiction**—of each level of government are set out in sections 91 to 93 of the BNA Act. Section 91 lists the powers of the federal government, while sections 92 and 93 list those of the provinces. Section 95 gives the federal and provincial governments shared powers over immigration and agriculture. Table 2.1 summarizes the division of powers.

division of powers
jurisdiction over major policy areas, as divided between the federal and the provincial governments

jurisdiction
sphere of influence or power

Section 92(8) gives the provinces the power to form municipalities and municipal governments. Section 93 gives the provinces control over education subject to certain clauses designed to safeguard the rights of Roman Catholic and Protestant minorities. Finally, although section 95 gives Parliament and the provincial legislatures shared power over agriculture and immigration, in case of conflict the federal government prevails.

Although there is much dispute today as to which level of government is most politically powerful, the terms of the BNA Act suggest that Canada's federal government was intended to be a strong authority. This is certainly true today, given the means of the federal government to raise

■ **Table 2.1   Division of Powers**

Federal Government	Provincial Governments
Section 91	**Section 92**
◆ Maintenance of peace, order, and good government	◆ Amendment of constitution of province, with the exception of office of lieutenant governor
◆ Public debt and property	◆ Direct taxation for provincial purposes
◆ Trade and commerce	◆ Borrowing of money on provincial credit
◆ Taxes	◆ Provincial government officers
◆ Borrowing money on the public credit	◆ Public lands belonging to the province
◆ Postal service	◆ Reformatories
◆ Census and statistics	◆ Hospital, asylums, and charities, other than marine hospitals
◆ Militia, military, and naval service, and defence	◆ Municipal institutions
◆ Setting of salaries of officers of the Government of Canada	◆ Shop, saloon, tavern, auctioneer, and other licences
◆ Beacons, buoys, lighthouses, and Sable Island	◆ Local works other than shipping lines, railways, canals, and telegraphs that connect provinces or extend beyond provincial borders
◆ Navigation and shipping	◆ Any works that, although they operate within a province are declared by the federal government to be for the general advantage of Canada or of two or more provinces
◆ Marine hospitals	
◆ Sea coast and inland fisheries	
◆ Ferries between a province and another country and between provinces	◆ Incorporation of companies operating only within a province
◆ Money	◆ Marriage ceremonies
◆ Banking	◆ Property and civil rights
◆ Weights and measures	◆ Provincial justice system
◆ Bills of exchange and promissory notes	◆ Imposition of fines, penalties, or imprisonment in enforcing provincial laws
◆ Interest	◆ Any matters of a local or private nature
◆ Patents	
◆ Copyrights	**Section 93**
◆ Aboriginal peoples and their lands	◆ Education
◆ Immigration	
◆ Marriage and divorce	
◆ Criminal law	
◆ Penitentiaries	

Federal and Provincial Governments

Section 95
◆ Agriculture and immigration are shared responsibilities

revenues through various forms of taxation and to determine how to return this money to the various provinces under strict conditions.

SUMMARY

Canada is a federation, a government structure that divides political powers between the federal and provincial governments. Confederation grew out of the desire of former British North American colonies to solve the problems posed by a small, scattered population characterized by geographic, cultural, and economic diversity. Our government structure represents an attempt to balance divergent interests for the overall public good. To this day, the challenges associated with such a balancing act—such as the demands of regional interests, bilingualism, Quebec's francophone culture, and First Nations' desire for self-government, to name only a few—continue to be the subjects of political debate.

KEY TERMS

Confederation

federal system

constitution

bicameral legislature

legislative union

division of powers

jurisdiction

NOTES

1. Margaret Conrad, Alvin Finkel, and Cornelius Jaenen, *History of the Canadian Peoples, Vol. 1: Beginnings to 1867* (Toronto: Copp Clark Pitman, 1993), 487.

2. *British North America Act, 1867*, 30-31 Vict., c. 3 (UK). Later renamed the *Constitution Act, 1867*. This will be discussed in detail in chapter 3.

3. Government of Nunavut, "The Road to Nunavut: A Chronological History," available at http://www.gov.nu.ca/eng/chronology.html.

EXERCISES

■ MULTIPLE CHOICE

1. The original members of Confederation were

   a. Canada West, Canada East, New Brunswick, and Newfoundland

   b. Canada West, Canada East, New Brunswick, and Nova Scotia

   c. Canada West, New Brunswick, Nova Scotia, and Prince Edward Island

   d. Canada East, Newfoundland, New Brunswick, and Nova Scotia

   e. Rupert's Land, Canada West, Canada East, and New Brunswick

2. Confederation promised

   a. economic advantages

   b. transportation advantages

   c. defence advantages

   d. trade advantages

   e. all of the above

3. The Canadian constitution, embodied in the BNA Act, borrowed from Britain

   a. a legislature composed of two Houses of Parliament

   b. the political party system

   c. the principle of responsible government

   d. b and c

   e. a, b, and c

4. A major departure of Canada from the British system of government was its structure as a

   a. unitary state

   b. legislative union

   c. constitutional monarchy

   d. federation

   e. all of the above

5. The powers of municipal, or local, governments are based in

   a. the constitution

   b. provincial powers to form and maintain local governments

   c. federal powers to form and maintain local governments

   d. all of the above

   e. none of the above

■ TRUE OR FALSE?

____ 1. Confederation offered transportation, trade, and defence advantages.

____ 2. A federal system of government gives all the power to the federal government.

____ 3. The BNA Act was the first statute passed by the Canadian government.

_____ 4. The new nation of Canada was a legislative union, a government structure borrowed from Britain.

_____ 5. The federal government is responsible for maintaining peace, order, and good government.

■ SHORT ANSWER

1. Define "federation."

2. What factors contributed to Canada's formation?

3. What did Confederation's supporters hope to achieve with this
union?

4. List some aspects of the Canadian political system that have their
roots in Britain.

5. Which aspect of Canada's political system was a major departure from Britain's?

6. If you could rewrite our constitution, how would you divide federal and provincial authority in the areas of justice and law enforcement? Explain.

CHAPTER 3

The Constitution and the Charter of Rights

CHAPTER OBJECTIVES

After completing this chapter, you should be able to:

◆ Describe the history of the *Constitution Act, 1982*, including attempts to amend it.

◆ Explain the impact of the *Charter of Rights and Freedoms* on Canadians' individual and collective rights.

◆ Describe the role of the Canadian judicial system in the political and constitutional process.

INTRODUCTION

This chapter explains how our current constitution came to be, what that means for our political system, and why constitutional reform continues to be an objective of our federal and provincial governments. The chapter also discusses the significance of the *Charter of Rights and Freedoms* to Canadians in general and to our judicial system.

THE PATH TO PATRIATION

As chapter 2 explained, the constitution of Canada has its source in the *British North America Act* of 1867, the British statute that united the former British North American colonies to form the Dominion of Canada.

Because the Act was a British statute, Britain had the power to reject Canadian laws, pass laws that affected Canada, and interpret and amend (change) Canadian laws. Thus, when Britain declared war on Germany in 1914, Canada was automatically involved in World War I as well. The Canadian constitution could be amended only by Britain, so every time Canada's federal government wanted to amend the Act, it had to ask the British Parliament to pass legislation to do so.

Canada's considerable contribution to the Allied cause in World War I and its growing sense of nationhood caused many Canadians to view this arrangement as both embarrassing and obsolete. Britain, for its part, was happy to comply with a Canadian request for change.

After many years of discussion, Canada gained some legislative independence from Britain with the passing of the *Statute of Westminister*[1] in 1931. With this statute, Britain aimed to simplify relations with Canada and other members of the British Commonwealth. The statute formally gave Canada authority over its domestic and external affairs and limited the British Parliament to legislating for Canada only when requested to do so by the Canadian government. However, because the federal and provincial governments couldn't agree on a constitutional **amending formula**— a process for changing the BNA Act—Britain retained its authority over Canadian constitutional amendments.

amending formula
a legal process for changing the constitution

Over the ensuing years, various Canadian federal governments tried to reach agreement on an amending formula with the provincial provinces so that the constitution could finally be brought under the control of Canada. While prime ministers such as Lester Pearson and Pierre Trudeau argued for a strong central government, the provinces increasingly demanded more powers, which would entail constitutional reform (recall from chapter 2 that the BNA Act divided powers between the federal and provincial governments, with the federal government retaining the greatest power). Quebec, for example, demanded control over social programs and economic policies. The election in Quebec of the separatist Parti québécois in 1976, led by René Lévesque, gave greater urgency to these demands.

patriation
the process of removing the Canadian constitution from British control and bringing it under Canadian control

In 1981, after much debate, all provinces except Quebec reached agreement with Prime Minister Trudeau about **patriating** the constitution —bringing it under Canadian control—an amending formula, and a charter of rights. Part of the provinces' agreement was based on being given more powers over their natural resources in the new constitution.

BRINGING THE CONSTITUTION HOME

It took another British statute, the *Canada Act* of 1982,[2] to patriate the Canadian constitution. The *Canada Act* confirmed that British legislation would no longer apply to Canada. Canada's new *Constitution Act, 1982*,[3] passed in April 1982, combines the old *British North America Act* (which was renamed the *Constitution Act, 1867*), the amending formula, and the *Charter of Rights and Freedoms*.[4] Unfortunately, Quebec refused to ratify (approve) the new constitution and, to date, has still not done so. Although it is not a signatory to the constitution, Quebec still benefits from and operates within the constitution of Canada.

The amending formula allows the federal government to change the constitution if it has the approval of Parliament and two-thirds (7 of 10) of the provinces that, combined, contain at least 50 percent of Canada's total population. Amendments that affect representation in the House of Commons, the Senate, and the Supreme Court and that affect the use of the French and English languages in government affairs require the consent of Parliament and all the provinces.[5]

The *Charter of Rights and Freedoms* (see appendix A) was the most significant amendment to the constitution, and will be discussed in more detail later in this chapter.

Despite patriation, Trudeau's vision of a unified Canada has yet to be realized. As the following sections will explain, close to two decades after patriation Canadians are still debating constitutional issues and attempting to win Quebec's signature to the constitution.

ONGOING CONSTITUTIONAL DEBATE

Two major attempts have been made since 1982 to amend the constitution to satisfy Quebec's main concerns as well as those of other provinces. In addition, women's groups, First Nations, and others have proposed constitutional amendments.

The Meech Lake Accord

An apparent agreement was reached between Prime Minister Brian Mulroney and the 10 provincial premiers at a first ministers' conference at Meech Lake, Ontario in April 1987. The proposed amendments of the Meech Lake Accord met Quebec's minimum demands:[6]

◆ Quebec would be recognized as a distinct society.

◆ Quebec would have a veto on any future constitutional changes.

◆ All provinces would have increased powers over immigration.

◆ All provinces would be able to opt out of any federal cost-sharing programs (for example, medicare and child care).

◆ Supreme Court of Canada judges would be appointed from lists provided by the provinces.

In addition, the concerns of the other provinces were addressed with the following:

◆ Provincial demands for Senate reform were met by giving the provinces the right to provide the federal government with a list of individuals from which to choose senators.

◆ Future constitutional amendments would be discussed at annual first ministers' meetings.

◆ All provinces—not just Quebec—would have the power to veto amendments.

Mulroney then announced that "no amendments to Meech Lake would be considered: it had to be ratified within three years by Parliament and by all ten provincial legislatures without a word changed."[7]

Despite the agreement of the politicians, many groups opposed the Meech Lake Accord. Some people were unhappy that ordinary Canadians had not been involved in the reform process in any way, arguing that the future of the nation should not be decided by only 11 men. People who were in favour of a strong federal government believed that the Accord gave too much power to the provinces. First Nations' hopes for a guarantee of the right to self-government were dashed. Many people, including Quebeckers, wanted to know exactly what "distinct society" meant in the legal sense, a definition that was not provided in the Accord. Many people were concerned about how this recognition of Quebec might affect the provisions of the *Charter of Rights* and how it would be interpreted by the Supreme Court when deciding issues related to the Charter. Mulroney countered that "distinct society" was mainly a symbolic term, thus basically confirming that it had little constitutional worth. Critics, many of them from Quebec, disagreed however. Other critics of the Accord included women's groups, groups worried that the ability of provinces to opt out of proposed shared-cost programs (for example, a national child-care program) would lead to the abandonment of such programs, and others.

Another stipulation of the Meech Lake Accord was that all provinces and the federal government were to ratify the agreement within three years—that is, pass a statute accepting the Accord in their respective Parliaments within three years. Three years passed and, with them, brought political party changes in several provinces. When the deadline was reached, 2 of the 10 provinces had still not approved the agreement: Newfoundland and Manitoba. Newfoundland Premier Clyde Wells, a lawyer and constitutional expert, was in favour of a strong federal government and an elected Senate with equal representation from all the provinces, and he was opposed to recognizing Quebec as a distinct society. In Manitoba, Member of the Legislative Assembly Elijah Harper, in a stand for First Nations rights, managed to delay a vote on the passage of the Accord.

The Meech Lake Accord died in 1990, as did hopes of obtaining Quebec's approval of the constitution. Quite the contrary—the debates surrounding Meech Lake had stirred up pro-separatist feelings. Quebeckers felt betrayed by the opposition to the distinct society clause and the switch from addressing Quebec's constitutional concerns to addressing the concerns of other groups. As a result, several Quebec members of the National Assembly formed a new federal political party—the Bloc québécois, led by one of Mulroney's most senior Cabinet ministers, Lucien Bouchard—to defend Quebec's rights in Ottawa. Quebec Premier Robert Bourassa announced plans for a referendum on separation for 1992. Facing growing support for Quebec separation, the federal and provincial leaders decided to resume negotiations toward a new accord before the referendum deadline.[8]

The Charlottetown Accord

The Charlottetown Accord of August 1992 was two years in the making and included something for everyone: special status for Quebec in exchange for equal provincial representation in the Senate, recognition of aboriginal rights to self-government, a social charter guaranteeing that existing social programs would be maintained by government, and more provincial powers. In addition, all Canadians would be involved in ratifying the Accord in a referendum scheduled for October 1992.

Despite polls suggesting that most Canadians would support the new Accord, 6 of the 10 provinces voted against it. It seemed that in trying to please everyone the Accord managed to please no one and only fuelled Quebec separatist sentiments. Everyone was tired of constitutional wrangles and wanted to turn to other pressing concerns, such as the serious economic recession and rising unemployment. Meanwhile, separatists in Quebec seized on Charlottetown as additional proof to back their cause. Quebec finally held its referendum on separation in 1995, which was only narrowly defeated when 49.4 percent of Quebeckers said "Yes" to separation from the rest of Canada.[9]

Recent Constitutional Issues

Canada has experienced some very difficult economic and social ills since the attempt to amend the *Constitution Act*. Constitutional issues and the threat of Quebec separation, although important, have taken a back seat to other priorities—jobs, health care, and the state of the economy among them. When Parti québécois leader Lucien Bouchard was re-elected premier of Quebec in 1998 with less than 43 percent of the popular vote, his government decided there was no pressing need for another referendum on separation. Meanwhile, the provinces and the federal government have continued to discuss various constitutional issues.

One result of negotiations was the Calgary Accord of September 1997, in which the federal government and all provinces except Quebec (which boycotted the meeting) agreed to a set of seven principles that, it was hoped, would bring Quebec into the constitution. Unlike the Meech Lake and Charlottetown accords, the Calgary Accord was mostly a goodwill gesture that expressed some general principles rather than specific constitutional amendments. For example, Quebec was described as having a unique character, but this was alongside statements about the diversity and equality of all the provinces. The Calgary Accord emphasized cooperation, multiculturalism, and the partnership between the federal and provincial/territorial governments. To date, little has come of this effort.

In the same year, the federal government decided to pursue the issue of separation through a Supreme Court challenge of Quebec's right to separate. The government asked the Supreme Court to address the questions of whether Quebec can legally make a unilateral decision to separate under the Canadian constitution (that is, decide on its own), whether Quebec can unilaterally separate under international law, and which law—Canadian or international—would apply if there were a conflict between the two.

In August 1998 the Supreme Court decided that Quebec had no unilateral right to separate under Canadian or international law, but also that the rest of Canada cannot deny Quebec's right to pursue separation if a majority of Quebeckers choose to do so. The court also decided that if a clear majority of Quebeckers voted for separation in a referendum, then the federal government has a "constitutional duty to negotiate" with Quebec. Note that the latter puts a reciprocal obligation on Quebec to negotiate.[10] After the Supreme Court ruling, the federal government introduced legislation in 1999 outlining how any separation vote must be conducted. The Quebec government countered with legislation of its own. The debate continues, as does the desire of some Quebeckers to secede.

THE CHARTER OF RIGHTS AND FREEDOMS

Charter of Rights and Freedoms

part of the Canadian constitution that guarantees certain fundamental rights and freedoms to all Canadians

common law

a body of law that has grown out of past court cases and is based on precedent or custom

As mentioned earlier in this chapter, probably the most significant aspect of the *Constitution Act, 1982* was the inclusion of the *Charter of Rights and Freedoms*. Since Confederation, Canadians had enjoyed rights such as freedom of speech under **common law** (law based on past legal decisions, or precedents) and custom, but these rights were not entrenched in the BNA Act. The Charter, the brainchild of then Prime Minister Pierre Trudeau, gave constitutional authority to a list of fundamental rights and freedoms enjoyed by all Canadians (see appendix A at the end of this book for the full text of the Charter).

With the addition of the Charter, Canada saw its government structure shed some of its British tradition—in which Parliament is the greatest power in the land—and take on more of the American tradition, where the Supreme Court is the highest power because of its right to interpret the terms of the constitution.[11] The Charter guarantees fundamental freedoms and democratic rights to all Canadians, thereby expressing the basic values of our nation, and sets out rules that all levels of government must follow.

Section 2 of the Charter sets out the fundamental freedoms:

◆ freedom of conscience and religion;

◆ freedom of thought, belief, opinion and expression, including freedom of the press and other media;

◆ freedom of peaceful assembly; and

◆ freedom of association.

The other sections set out various rights, declare Canada's official bilingualism, explain how rights and freedoms are enforced, and describe how the Charter applies to all levels of government. Sections 7–14 set out legal rights, which are particularly relevant to law enforcement, some of which include

◆ the right to life, liberty, and security of the person;

◆ the right to be secure against unreasonable search and seizure;

◆ the right not to be arbitrarily detained or imprisoned;

◆ on arrest or detention, the right to be informed promptly of the reason for arrest and the specific offence;

◆ the right to retain counsel;

◆   the right to be tried within a reasonable time; and

◆   the right to be presumed innocent until proven guilty.

The Charter is a fundamental piece of legislation that law enforcement officers need to understand and conscientiously apply. As part of the constitution, the Charter must be considered in concert with other Canadian criminal and civil laws and also applies to the actions of government and its representatives, such as law enforcement officers. Thus, anyone who believes that Charter rights are being contravened by any federal or provincial law can dispute that law in court and, conceivably, have it struck down as unconstitutional by the court. Similarly, if a court finds that an accused person's rights have been contravened at any step in the judicial process by any agent of the state—such as law enforcement officers—the charge against the accused may be stayed.

Limits on Charter Rights

Included within the Charter's guarantees of rights are some limits to those rights. We will discuss two of the most important qualifiers here. First is the "reasonable limits" clause in section 1:

> 1. The *Canadian Charter of Rights and Freedoms* guarantees the rights and freedoms set out in it subject only to such reasonable limits prescribed by law as can be demonstrably justified in a free and democratic society.

This means that Charter rights can be overridden if the government can prove that an apparent Charter violation is a reasonable limit. For example, when police officers conduct a RIDE (Reduce Impaired Driving Everywhere) program, they are allowed to detain motorists because doing so is seen as a reasonable limit that can prevent motorists and others from harm caused by drunk drivers. Similarly, the right of freedom of speech does not extend to spreading hate literature against a particular person or group in our society.

The "notwithstanding clause" in section 33 is another limit in the Charter, and one that has been the subject of much controversy.

> 33. (1) Parliament or the legislature of a province may expressly declare in an Act of Parliament or of the legislature, as the case may be, that the Act or a provision thereof shall operate notwithstanding a provision included in section 2 or sections 7 to 15 of this Charter.

What this means is that a government can override a section of the Charter with one of its own laws by passing legislation declaring that it is doing so. Section 33 goes on to explain the time limits on such an action. This clause seems to have been a way for Trudeau to secure the provincial premiers' approval of the Charter. Shortly after the passage of the constitution in 1982 Quebec used the notwithstanding clause to exempt all of its legislation from the Charter, claiming that its provincial human rights code protected Quebeckers adequately. This has allowed Quebec to, for example, override the minority-language education rights that are set out in section 23 of the Charter.

An Expanded Role for the Courts

The Charter has effectively shifted some power from the government to the courts, whose role now includes interpreting the impact of any legislation on Charter rights. Individuals as well as special-interest groups are challenging legislation and government policy in ways that were not possible before 1982. What were once political issues are increasingly becoming legal issues, and some people see this new power of the courts —and of the people who challenge the Charter—as dangerous. In a democratic system that is based on representatives elected by citizens, should unelected judges have the right to overturn laws and policies made by our elected representatives?

This question is a complex one that has no simple answer, and it is being hotly debated by academics, lawyers, concerned citizens, and others. Some believe that the courts, particularly the Supreme Court of Canada, have too much political power, while others believe that this new role of the courts is exactly what is needed to make sure our politicians uphold the laws of the land, including the rights of citizens.

SUMMARY

More than 100 years after Confederation, Canada finally brought home its constitution in 1982. The central documents of our current *Constitution Act, 1982* are the *British North America Act*, now called the *Constitution Act, 1867*, and the *Canadian Charter of Rights and Freedoms*. However, we are still struggling as a nation to reach a consensus on many related issues and particularly to get Quebec's signature to the constitution.

Several attempts have been made to incorporate the conditions that Quebec believes are necessary prerequisites to signing the constitution. These attempts included the Meech Lake and Charlottetown accords, both of which failed to win the support of a majority of provinces. Attempts at constitutional reform continue, but have taken a back seat to other issues in recent years.

The *Charter of Rights and Freedoms* has significance in our everyday lives and in the institutions of government. The Charter enshrines rights and freedoms in the constitution that previously existed only as part of Canadian common law and custom. As a result, it has had significant implications for our political system, particularly in terms of the increased power of the judiciary, which has, many argue, become a third branch of government (a topic that will be discussed in more detail in chapter 4).

KEY TERMS

amending formula

patriation

Charter of Rights and Freedoms

common law

NOTES

1. *Statute of Westminster,* 22 George V, c. 4 (1931).

2. *Canada Act, 1982* (UK), c. 11 (1982).

3. *Constitution Act, 1982,* RSC 1985, app. II, no. 44.

4. *Canadian Charter of Rights and Freedoms,* part I of the *Constitution Act, 1982,* RSC 1985, app. II, no. 44.

5. Alvin Finkel and Margaret Conrad, with Veronica Strong-Boag, *History of the Canadian Peoples, Vol. 2: 1867 to the Present* (Toronto: Copp Clark Pitman, 1993), 585.

6. Ronald H. Wagenberg, "The Institutions of the Canadian State," in Kenneth G. Pryke and Walter C. Soderlund, eds., *Profiles of Canada* (Toronto: Copp Clark Pitman, 1992), 102.

7. Finkel and Conrad, with Strong-Boag, 593.

8. Ibid., 592–98.

9. Ibid., 598–602.

10. Warren J. Newman, *The Quebec Secession Reference: The Rule of Law and the Position of the Attorney General of Canada* (Toronto: York University, 1999), ch. 4.

11. Wagenberg, 112.

EXERCISES

∎ MULTIPLE CHOICE

1. Since 1982, government constitutional negotiations have centred on

   a. redefining federal and provincial government powers

   b. obtaining Quebec's signature to the *Constitution Act, 1982*

   c. reforming the Senate

   d. addressing the concerns of various groups in Canadian society

   e. all of the above

2. The Charter is a significant part of our constitution because it

    a. changed the Canadian political system from one based in British tradition to a system more like that of the United States

    b. is above all other law

    c. enshrines specific rights for all Canadians

    d. limits government legislation and policies

    e. all of the above

3. The rights and freedoms set out in the Charter

    a. can be limited by the federal and provincial governments

    b. can be limited by the "reasonable limits" and "notwithstanding" clauses

    c. have no limits

    d. can be limited by the courts

    e. a and b

4. The Charter of Rights is relevant to law enforcement because it

    a. defines the rights of citizens, including those of persons accused of committing offences

    b. limits the actions of government and its agents in maintaining public order

    c. gives law enforcement officers the right to decide what constitutes reasonable limits on citizens' behaviour

    d. all of the above

    e. a and b

5. The expanded role of the Canadian courts since the passing of the Charter is controversial because now

    a. the courts are more powerful than the government

    b. unelected judges interpret the Charter and make decisions that affect laws and policies created by elected politicians

    c. the courts are responsible for making laws

    d. the court can overturn any law or policy they don't like

    e. all of the above

∎ TRUE OR FALSE?

_____ 1. Under the BNA Act, the Canadian government simply passed legislation when it wanted to amend the Act.

_____ 2. Canada's current constitution is called the *Canada Act*.

_____ 3. Before the *Charter of Rights and Freedoms* was added to the constitution, Canadians enjoyed rights under common law and by custom.

_____ 4. The Charter has no effect on the justice system or on how law enforcement officers do their job.

_____ 5. The Charter grants unlimited fundamental rights and freedoms to all Canadians.

∎ SHORT ANSWER

1. Explain why Quebec has not signed the *Constitution Act, 1982*. What are its main concerns?

2. In order to amend the constitution, what has to happen first?

3. Why have the federal and provincial governments attempted constitutional reform? What are they trying to achieve?

4. List some advantages and disadvantages of having a powerful judiciary as part of our political structure.

5. Describe how the *Charter of Rights and Freedoms* affects you now and will affect you in a future career in law enforcement.

CHAPTER 4

Welcome to the Machine: Canadian Political Structure and Its Operation

CHAPTER OBJECTIVES

After completing this chapter, you should be able to:

◆ Define and differentiate the terms "representative government" and "responsible government."

◆ Understand the structure and roles of the three levels of government.

◆ Explain how laws are enacted at the three levels of government.

◆ Describe the status of First Nations within our political structure.

WHAT IS REPRESENTATIVE GOVERNMENT?

Imagine for a moment that your college has decided to allow students to decide what colour to paint the classrooms. What is the most democratic way the institution could arrive at a decision? Your response might be "Ask every student." This sounds straightforward, but in schools where enrollment is literally in the thousands it would take a very long time, and worse, some students might change their minds. Further, by the time the entire student body had been consulted the year might be over, with an entirely new group of students arriving in the fall. In short, democracy taken to an extreme is simply too time-consuming and achieves little in the way of results.

Now, what is the most efficient way to achieve this same goal? Well, you could decide based on your individual preference, but this would be seen as blatantly undemocratic and would therefore lack the support of your fellow students. Another solution is to select a number of students—say one from each program—to poll their respective peers and bring the results to a meeting where a vote could be held on each colour. In this way, democratic consultation and administrative efficiency would be accommodated to an acceptable degree. Voilà! You have just created a representative system of consultation. Representative government works on the very same principle.

41

representative government
government that is based on members elected by citizens to represent their interests

    Representative government is one in which people are elected from each geographic area to represent the concerns of the people living in that area. It is a fundamental principle of democracy. Canada has a representative government that is based on members elected by citizens to represent their interests. Similarly, the provincial and territorial governments have members elected by citizens to represent their interests. We will explain these government structures in detail in this chapter.

Elections in Canada

In Canada, elections are called at the discretion of the prime minister at the federal level, and at the discretion of the premiers at the provincial level. In both cases, an election must take place no later than five years following the last election. Municipal election schedules vary from province to province. Ontario municipalities have elections every three years.

    One of the major players in an election is the candidate who is running for office. (The other major player, the constituent or voter, is discussed in chapter 11.) The rules and regulations governing candidacy are contained in the *Canada Elections Act*[1] and its counterparts at the provincial and territorial levels. With a few exceptions, the rules are very similar. You must be a resident of Canada and be eligible to vote. You cannot currently be serving as a political representative at another level, and you must be innocent of any previous corrupt political practices for the previous five years. You are also disqualified if you are imprisoned or are an election officer. Most judges and some Crown attorneys are also prohibited from running.[2] Federal candidates must collect 100 signatures of fellow electors and make a deposit of $1,000. In Ontario, the same number of signatures is required but the fee is $200, and for municipal elections, no signatures are required and the fee is $100.[3]

WHAT IS RESPONSIBLE GOVERNMENT?

The concept of responsible government is another central principle characterizing democratic countries such as Canada, where the system of government is based on a parliamentary model. The principle of **responsible government** requires that the government may govern only as long as it has the support of a majority of the state's elected representatives.

responsible government
government that is responsible to the wishes of its citizens, as embodied in their elected representatives

Majority or Minority?

If a majority votes against the government on an issue of major importance, then that government must resign, thus dissolving Parliament. In almost all cases, this results in an election call to allow voters to decide which party will form the next government. In Canada's House of Commons, for example, a simple majority of 151 **members of Parliament** (MPs) voting against a major government bill would trigger this event.

member of Parliament
an elected representative in the House of Commons who represents a riding

In reality, however, this rarely happens because of another parliamentary tradition called party loyalty. **Party loyalty** demands that all members of a particular political party vote according to the wishes of their leader. In other words, they are not free to vote as they wish. This means that as long as the government—that is, the political party with the most elected representatives—can convince 151 or more MPs in the House of Commons to vote in its favour, it can continue to hold power.

Observing the principle of responsible government is particularly easy when 151 or more MPs belong to the same party. In this situation the party forms what is called a **majority government**, since its members constitute a majority in the legislature. But what happens when a federal political party ends up with more MPs but fails to achieve the number required for a majority? In this case, a **minority government** is formed. As you can probably tell, minority governments are much more unstable because opposition MPs outnumber, and can therefore outvote, the government on any issue.

There are advantages and disadvantages to each situation. Majority governments are much more productive in terms of the amount of legislation they produce because they can outvote opposition members as a bill makes its way through the legislative process (discussed later in this chapter). They also don't need to worry about losing their mandate through an opposition-sponsored non-confidence vote—a vote to replace the government because it has lost the confidence of the majority of the House. Thus, majority governments are free to decide when the next election will be held. This power is limited somewhat by the fact that in Canada a party in power must call an election no later than five years after the last one (although there are exceptions to this rule in times of public emergency, such as war or domestic crises). Most governments typically wait about four years before issuing an election call. Majority governments are often criticized for being insensitive to viewpoints that are different from those of their party, and may be perceived by constituents as arrogant and undemocratic.

Minority governments face almost the opposite set of challenges. They are forced to listen to opposition concerns, which often leads to political compromises or further consideration. But this situation also makes minority governments inherently unproductive and short-lived. The cooperative consultative practices inherent in minority governments can bog down the legislative process, and the opposition parties may outvote—and thus defeat—the government at any time. The result is a very unpredictable session. Historically, Canadians have tended to vote in majority governments, the last minority government being elected in 1979. True to form, this minority government, led by Joe Clark, lasted less than a year—from May 1979 to February 1980—before it was defeated.

party loyalty
the requirement that all members of a political party vote according to the wishes of their leader

majority government
a government that includes more than half of the total MPs in the House of Commons (in 2000, this required 151 MPs of a total of 301)

minority government
a government that has the greatest number of MPs in the House of Commons but not more than half of the total MPs

STRUCTURE OF THE FEDERAL GOVERNMENT

In democratic countries such as Canada, power is usually separated into three main categories: executive, legislative, and judicial. We can think of the organization of the federal government in terms of these three branches (see figure 4.1).

The Executive Branch

executive branch (federal)
the branch of government that includes the monarch's representative (governor general), the elected head of state (prime minister), and Cabinet

The **executive branch** of the federal government includes the Queen (or current reigning British monarch), the governor general (the Queen's representative in Canada), the prime minister, Cabinet, and the ministries and departments that provide government goods and services. In a parliamentary system, the power to govern rests here.

Although officially Canada's head of state, the Queen in reality has no role in Canadian government except to formally appoint the governor general, who is always chosen by the prime minister. The governor general acts as the Queen's representative in Canada, although the relationship is entirely ceremonial in nature, hearkening back to our colonial ties to the British empire. The governor general mainly performs functions such as opening Parliament, and she or he is usually appointed for a term of five years.

The prime minister (PM) and Cabinet are the most important members of the executive branch and the people we usually think of as "government." The real locus of power lies here. As leader of the national party in power, the prime minister wields considerable power within this structure. He or she controls the appointment of Cabinet ministers, deputy ministers, senators, senior judges, and a host of other important government positions. He or she also has the power to dissolve Parliament, which results in an election call.

Cabinet
the government body that consists of MPs appointed by the prime minister who oversee government departments and act as advisers in major policy areas

The **Cabinet**—chaired by the PM—is where government policies are developed, debated, and decided. Cabinet is made up of MPs selected by the prime minister to represent the diverse population of the country. Cabinet ministers oversee individual government departments, communicating the political will of the Cabinet as it applies to each department.

Cabinet solidarity
the united front that Cabinet presents on given policy matters, although individual Cabinet ministers may privately be opposed

While individual Cabinet ministers may privately disagree with government policies, they are bound to support government action publicly. This reflects the principle of **Cabinet solidarity**, which allows the government to speak with one voice on given policy matters. The bureaucracy, or civil service, is responsible for implementing political will, and will be examined in detail in part III of this text.

The Legislative Branch

legislative branch (federal)
the lawmaking branch of government (House of Commons and Senate)

Lawmaking is a major government role, and most legislation, or law, is the result of government initiatives that are designed to carry out election promises. The **legislative branch** consists of those government bodies

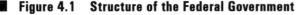

■ **Figure 4.1   Structure of the Federal Government**

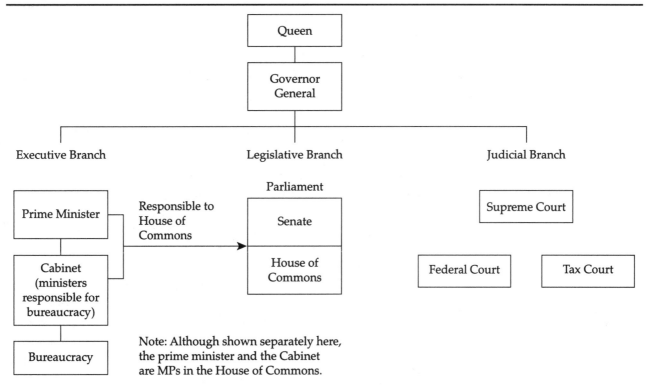

that are responsible for passing legislation. At the federal level, this branch includes the two Houses of Parliament: the House of Commons (the lower chamber) and the Senate (the upper chamber).

Proceedings in each chamber are overseen by the Speaker, who is elected from among the current MPs, or in the case of the Senate, selected by the prime minister. Once in that position, the Speaker assumes a neutral, non-partisan role, maintaining order and ensuring respect for the rules of Parliament.

House of Commons

In 2000 the House of Commons was made up of 301 MPs representing the 301 geographic areas—called ridings or constituencies—into which Canada has been divided. Ridings vary in size according to population, with each containing approximately 100,000 Canadians. When an election is held, candidates in each riding compete to get the most voter support. The candidate with the most votes becomes the MP for that riding.

The party with the second-highest number of MPs elected forms the Official Opposition. These MPs, along with the other non-government members of the House, hold the governing party publicly accountable and responsible for its actions. They also participate in passing legislation and represent their respective constituencies.

Senate

There are 105 seats in the Senate (as of 2000). Senators, who are appointed by the prime minister rather than elected, approve decisions of the House of Commons (the process is explained in more detail later in this chapter). Senators must be at least 30 years old, and they may hold office until age 75. There are 24 senators from each of Ontario and Quebec; 6 from each of BC, Alberta, Saskatchewan, and Manitoba; 10 from each of New Brunswick and Nova Scotia; 6 from Newfoundland; 4 from PEI; and 1 from each of the territories.

triple E Senate
a Senate that is equal, elected, and effective

The chamber of "sober second thought" has come under increasing criticism in recent times because its members are not elected and are therefore not directly accountable to the Canadian public. As well, the Senate has become a patronage reward for friends of the prime minister and those loyal to his or her party. A general perception exists that as long as senators are appointed, this House has no legitimacy. This has led to calls for what has become known as a **triple E Senate**—one that is equal, elected, and effective. The logic is that, if an equal number of senators were elected from each province, then the Senate would function as it was originally intended and its integrity would thereby be restored. So far, no prime minister has been willing to make this change, but discussion about Senate reform will likely continue.

How Federal Law Is Made

bill
a proposed law

A proposed law is called a **bill**. There are three different kinds of bills: government, private member's, and private. All bills are not created equal—successful navigation through Parliament's legislative labyrinth depends to a large extent on who has sponsored the voyage.

government bill
a bill proposed by a member of Cabinet

Government bills are introduced by Cabinet members and concern national matters. Only this category of bill can involve spending public money or imposing taxes. Not surprisingly, government bills almost always pass. This is because the legislation in question has the support of the governing party, which can take advantage of the principle of party loyalty to ensure passage.

private member's bill
a bill proposed by a non-Cabinet MP

Private members' bills are sponsored by either backbench MPs (members of the governing party who do not sit in Cabinet) or opposition MPs. These bills are normally used to propose an alternative to existing government policy or to embarrass the government into action, so they are usually defeated or sidelined by the governing party. It is only because of parliamentary reforms that these bills are even allowed to be discussed. If a private member's bill ever hopes to pass into law it must have strong public support and relate to a national concern. For example, for years some people have believed that Canada should have a national holiday in February called Heritage Day. Every now and then a private member's bill surfaces to propose such a holiday.

private bill
a bill proposed by a senator

Private bills are always introduced in the Senate and almost always pass. They deal with minor issues, such as professional designations, that

■ **Figure 4.2   A Federal Bill Becomes Law**

First Reading

Bill is introduced by a minister in House of Commons. Bill is printed and copies are given to all MPs.

Second Reading

MPs debate bill and take vote on its general principles. If it passes, bill is referred to a committee.

Committee Stage

Bill is examined in detail by a committee made up of MPs. Committee may get experts to provide information related to bill and help improve it.

Report Stage

Committee returns bill and proposed amendments to House of Commons. MPs debate and vote on amendments.

Third Reading

House of Commons debates and votes on bill as amended.

Senate Approval

Bill goes through same process in Senate. If amended by Senate, bill returns to House of Commons to be passed again.

Royal Assent

Governor general approves bill, and it becomes law.

concern a person or a group of people—for example, authorizing the Canadian Institute of Chartered Accountants to use the professional designation of chartered accountant.

The overwhelming power of a governing party to control the legislative process has caused many MPs and members of the public to criticize this practice and has led to some parliamentary reform, but the Cabinet remains a dominant force in setting the legislative agenda.

The various kinds of bills must all pass through Parliament and be approved before becoming law. Figure 4.2 summarizes the process. Note that the final step, royal assent, is only a formality since the governor general's role is merely ceremonial and carries no political power.

Judicial Branch

Courts exist to enforce the principle of the rule of law. This means that all government actions must be authorized by law and there must be specific legal authority for the actions taken by government. As explained in chapter 1, this principle is essential to our democratic system and ensures that no government official is above the law.

judicial branch
the branch of government that consists of the court system

The **judicial branch** of government basically consists of the court system, which helps to legitimize the rule of law and also supports the powers of the federal and provincial governments as identified in the *Constitution Act*.[4] At the federal level, the judicial branch consists of the Supreme Court of Canada, the Federal Court of Canada, and the Tax Court of Canada.

The Supreme Court consists of nine judges, including the Chief Justice, who are appointed by the federal government. Three judges must come from Quebec, but appointment of the rest is based only on custom: three are usually from Ontario, two from the West, and one from the Atlantic provinces. The judges may serve until they are 75 years old.

The Supreme Court is the final court of appeal in Canada, and its decisions are binding on all the lower courts, including those of the provinces. The Supreme Court also serves a political purpose in that it facilitates the operation of the federal system by deciding which level—federal or provincial—has constitutional jurisdiction, in addition to upholding individual and group rights guaranteed under the *Charter of Rights and Freedoms*.[5] In recent years, the Supreme Court has increasingly been hearing Charter challenges—that is, cases that deal with alleged violations of Charter rights and alleged unconstitutional legislation and government policy. One famous case in this regard has involved the legal right of Quebec to separate from Canada (discussed in chapter 3).

Supreme Court decisions, which are separate from and independent of government, occasionally force governments to either withdraw or modify proposed legislation, or to compensate individuals and groups whose constitutional rights have been violated. For example, in the past prisoners were not allowed to vote in elections. Since the passage of the Charter in 1982, which lists voting as a democratic right of Canadian citizens, prisoners have successfully challenged the denial of this basic right and won the right to vote.

The Federal Court hears cases concerning such areas as federal taxes, patents, and copyrights. The Tax Court hears appeals on cases that concern the *Income Tax Act*,[6] the Canada Pension Plan, the goods and services tax, and so on.

STRUCTURE OF THE PROVINCIAL GOVERNMENTS

The structure of the provincial governments is parallel to that of the federal government, with the notable exception that there is no upper chamber in the legislative branch. It can be divided into the same three branches (see figure 4.3 for Ontario's government structure).

Executive Branch

At the provincial level, the **executive branch** includes the lieutenant governor (who represents the Queen), the premier (called the "prime minister" in Quebec), and Cabinet (called the Executive Council in Ontario). The lieutenant governor is formally appointed by the governor general, but the prime minister actually chooses the person for this position. Again, the lieutenant governor's role is mostly ceremonial (for example, he or she opens the Legislative Assembly), and key political decisions are made by the premier and Cabinet.

executive branch (provincial) *the branch of government that includes the monarch's representative (lieutenant governor), the elected head of state (premier), and Cabinet*

The three territories are officially administered by the federal government, which is represented by a commissioner for each territory. In reality, the commissioner has much the same role as that of the lieutenant governor of a province. The territories each have an elected Legislative Assembly made up of a premier and MLAs, but these governments operate based on consensus rather than on party-based confrontation. The premier and Cabinet are chosen by fellow MLAs by secret ballot.

Legislative Branch

The provincial **legislative branch** is called the National Assembly in Quebec and the Legislative Assembly in all other provinces. The provincial governments differ from the federal government in that they have a unicameral (or one-House) legislature. The Legislative Assembly has its counterpart in the federal House of Commons, but no upper chamber that corresponds to the Senate.

legislative branch (provincial) *the lawmaking branch of government (Legislative/National Assembly)*

Elected representatives of provincial governments are known as members of the provincial Parliament (MPPs) in Ontario, members of the Legislative Assembly (MLAs) in other provinces except Quebec, and members of the National Assembly (MNAs) in Quebec. The number of sitting members in each of the provinces and territories varies in propor-

■ Figure 4.3   Structure of the Ontario Government

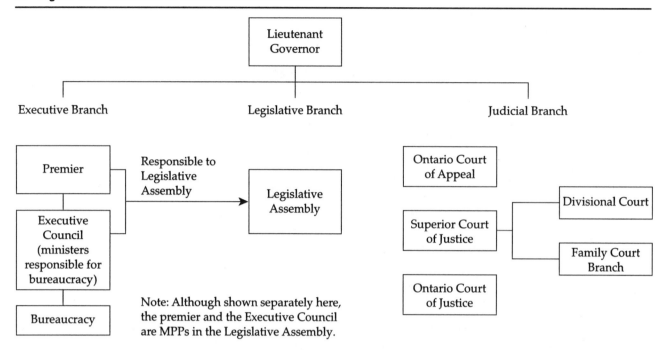

Note: Although shown separately here, the premier and the Executive Council are MPPs in the Legislative Assembly.

tion to the population of the province or territory. In 2000, Ontario had 103 MPPs.

How Provincial Law Is Made

The legislative assemblies of the provinces pass laws using much the same process as the federal Parliament, except that there is no provincial equivalent to the Senate: three readings, a committee stage, final debate, final vote, and royal assent by the lieutenant governor. Government bills concern provincial matters and are introduced by Cabinet ministers. Private members' bills also concern provincial matters and are introduced by any other MPP. Private bills usually concern a person or corporation and can be introduced by any MPP, but are often introduced by the MPP for the particular person or corporation's riding.[7]

Judicial Branch

This branch of government consists of the provincial courts, which do not have any real political power but uphold the laws made by the legislative branch. The judicial branch structure varies from province to province, so the names of individual courts and divisions also vary. Each province has a Superior or Supreme Court that has trial and appeal divisions. The trial division often includes small claims, family, and other courts. There may also be civil and criminal divisions. As well as the Superior Court there are provincial courts, which may also include family, small claims, youth, and other courts. Judges are appointed by the provinces.[8]

STRUCTURE OF MUNICIPAL GOVERNMENTS

The third level of government is municipal or local government. As mentioned in chapter 2, the Canadian constitution gives the provinces the responsibility for municipal governments—the municipalities themselves have no constitutional powers. It is at each province's discretion whether to create local governments and also what responsibilities municipal governments will have. Usually, local governments are responsible for such services as roads, police, firefighting, sewers, water, garbage collection, and so on. Schools are usually maintained separately by a school board. In Ontario, local governments are managed by a provincial law called the *Municipal Act.*[9]

Because municipal governments are a provincial responsibility, their structure varies widely. However, most tend to have a simple structure that includes only one elected body of representatives (generally with no political party affiliation)—the **municipal council**—which combines legislative and executive roles. Typically the municipal government consists of this council and its staff. The size of the council depends on the size of the municipality. There are several categories of municipality: city, town, village, rural municipality, county, or regional, district, or metropolitan municipality. Some councils have as few as 3 members, while in 2000 Toronto's had 44 members. Generally a mayor heads the council, although he or she may also be a reeve (in rural municipalities), a warden (in a county), or a chair (in a regional municipality). Council members are elected by ward (the municipal equivalent of a riding) and are known as aldermen or councillors (the term "aldermen" is falling out of favour since many are women). Municipal governments pass local laws, called **bylaws**, as well as supervise local services and hire staff for those services.

municipal council
the governing body of a municipal government

In recent years several provinces have taken measures to reduce the number of municipalities in an effort to cut costs and reduce duplication of services. Ontario is one province that is significantly reducing the number of municipalities, as witnessed by the formation of the Toronto "megacity" by amalgamating seven municipal governments in 1997.

bylaw
a local or municipal law

Councils can appoint citizens to various committees to make decisions on specific responsibilities, such as local roads, recreation, libraries, water, sewers, garbage collection, firefighting, police protection, public transportation, and so on. The day-to-day running of the local government is generally handled by staff that is organized into various departments, which are managed by department heads reporting to either a clerk or chief administrative officer (CAO) of the municipality. The departments, for example, could be the recreation department, public works (water, sewers, and roads), fire department, and so on. The clerk or CAO reports directly to council (see figure 4.4).

Local governments can be a major contributing factor to our quality of life since they are responsible for administering the services and programs we enjoy every day. In recent years some provincial governments have downloaded more and more responsibility for services to local governments without making sure they have adequate money to provide these

■ Figure 4.4   Example of a Municipal Government Structure

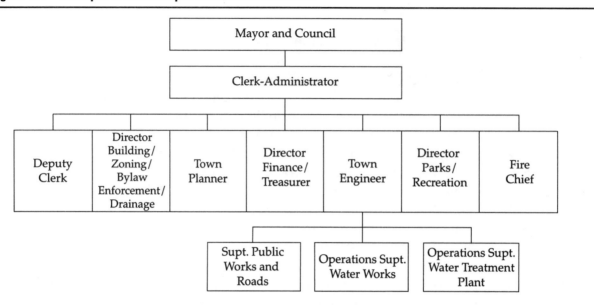

Source: Reprinted with permission from *Bradford West Gwillimbury Community Profile* (Town of Bradford West Gwillimbury, 1998), p. 7.

services. Examples of areas in which this downloading has occurred include local roads, transportation, public housing, and emergency services such as ambulance. Unfortunately, despite their importance in our everyday lives, local governments are rarely given the credit and attention they deserve.

How Municipal Bylaws Are Made

The process of passing bylaws is not nearly as complicated as the process of passing federal and provincial laws. The municipal council votes on bylaws proposed by its members and staff of the municipality and passes those that have the support of a majority of council members.

FIRST NATIONS IN THE CANADIAN POLITICAL STRUCTURE

Members of First Nations in Canada have a unique, and many would say extremely disadvantaged, status in our current political structure.

In chapter 2, in the section on the division of powers, you may have noticed that aboriginal peoples came under federal jurisdiction. Otherwise, the *British North America Act* made no mention of First Nations. In recent decades Canadians have witnessed First Nations' growing frustration with government, sometimes erupting into violent confrontations when peaceful negotiations have been unsuccessful. The idea of aboriginal self-government has been steadily gaining support and has been instituted in parts of Canada (for example, Nunavut). This topic will be discussed further in chapter 5, but here we will briefly discuss some of the relevant history and context of the First Nations' relationship with the federal government and the rest of Canada.

A First Nation is legally identified as a "band" under the *Indian Act* if it possesses three qualities: a reserve base-land, government trust funds for its use, and has been declared a band by the federal government. ... (Note: The federal government does not recognize the term "First Nations" but identifies Native communities as "Bands." ...)[10]

Keep in mind as you read this section that the term "First Nations" covers diverse peoples, cultures, and traditions, and that it is dangerous —as well as naive—to assume that all these groups are the same and have the same goals. "Canada has 633 First Nations communities within its borders."[11] As well, since detailed coverage of the status of First Nations in the Canadian political structure is beyond the scope of this book, this section greatly simplifies the history and issues that have led to their current status.

Historical Background

The history of First Nations since colonial times is a history of steady erosion of their rights and independence and of broken promises on the part of government. When the European colonists no longer needed the First Nations' help in war and trade, they began to see these peoples as liabilities and obstacles to expansion and development. Government initiatives in relation to aboriginal peoples turned to assimilating them into the non-aboriginal culture and "protecting" Native land by creating and controlling reserves on which aboriginal peoples were to live. With the *Royal Proclamation of 1763*, Britain attempted to organize its newly acquired territory in North America after the defeat of the French in 1760. In this statute, the British government declared itself the only party that could make treaties with the aboriginal peoples, and it also set down a treaty-making process.[12]

After the new Canadian government was given responsibility for aboriginal peoples under the BNA Act, it passed the *Indian Act*[13] in 1876, a statute that confirmed its control over their lands, the resources on those lands, and the lives of the people themselves. Until the passing of this Act, First Nations had governed themselves and made their own decisions. Under the Act, the federal government imposed changes on how chiefs and councils were to operate, how bands were to select their leaders, and so on—basically, the government dismissed First Nations customs and replaced them with laws that were made without consulting the people they affected.[14] In addition, First Nations peoples were subject to the legislation of the province in which they resided.

The Act covered only registered or status Indians—the descendants of those people who were considered Indians when the Act was passed, a definition that excluded the Métis and Inuit peoples. Status Indians were entitled to certain services provided by the federal government (in the areas of health, education, and so on), but they could not vote in federal elections until 1961, when this condition was finally changed. Status could also be lost, as we will discuss below, with the result that some people were and still are excluded from the Act.

Revisions to the *Indian Act* in 1951 further restricted who was eligible for status. Status Indian women who married non-status men—even men of aboriginal ancestry—automatically lost their status. The same condition did not apply to men who married non-status women. Losing status meant losing certain federal services, losing any private property on a reserve, and even losing the right to live on the reserve. This discriminatory condition was abolished in 1985 after much protest, and some First Nations members have regained their status.[15]

Over the years there have been many revisions to the *Indian Act*, but it continues to apply only to those people defined by the government as status Indians. It is no longer possible for status Indians to lose their status. You might think First Nations people would welcome an end to the status Indian category, but in fact most oppose abolishing it because doing so would lead only to more hardship for people who already face much higher levels of poverty, unemployment, and other socioeconomic problems in relation to the non-aboriginal population.

Treaties

In addition to federal statutes, First Nations' rights are based in their historical occupation of the land and in treaties signed with first the British and then the Canadian governments. These treaties—agreements between First Nations bands and the government of the day—first established peace and trade between the parties, and later increasingly involved transferring land to the government. With this loss of land—and the livelihood they made from this land—First Nations lost much of their autonomy.

Treaties fall into three main categories: pre-Confederation treaties, numbered treaties, and modern treaties. Pre-Confederation treaties were made with the British government before Canada became a nation. Many of the original documents have been lost or were poorly recorded. Eleven numbered treaties were made between 1871 and 1921 as Canada grew as a nation and built a national railway, and these required First Nations to accept settlement on reserves. Most of these treaties also promised the First Nations schools, farming equipment, money, and other benefits, many of which never materialized. Modern treaties are land claim agreements that have been signed since 1973.[16]

As you can imagine, the result is a patchwork of treaties across Canada, some of them dating back to the 1700s. Many of the promises made by the government have never been fulfilled, although government initiated the treaties, but the treaties continue to be recognized as legal documents by our judicial system. Treaty disputes continue to today and must be resolved on a treaty-by-treaty basis. Individual treaties are not always clear about the rights and responsibilities they confer. Further complicating matters: some treaties contradict provincial regulations, written treaty provisions must be interpreted, unwritten promises that have survived as oral history have to be considered, and some provisions have since been overridden by federal legislation—and these are only some of the factors that make settling disputes over land, aboriginal rights, and other issues so complex.[17]

Funding

Most of the funding for services and programs provided to First Nations comes from the federal government, the majority of it from the Department of Indian Affairs and Northern Development. Some examples include educational programs (for example, band schools, First Nations culture and language programs), health care programs (for example, alcohol and drug awareness, mental health), child welfare, and economic development (for example, support for small businesses). Over the years, First Nations bands have been given more and more control over the day-to-day administration of these services, services that other Canadians receive through their provincial and municipal governments. However, funding for many First Nations programs, such as in the area of health care, still lags behind the level of funding other Canadians enjoy.[18]

First Nations Rights

It is clear that the government's attempts over the years to assimilate First Nations into the non-aboriginal population have failed.[19] Distinct Native groups still exist across Canada, just as the non-Native population is made up of distinct ethnic groups. After many years of resistance to and criticism of federal policy regarding First Nations, in 1982 the aboriginal and treaty rights of Indians, Inuit, and Métis were enshrined in 1982 in the *Charter of Rights and Freedoms* (section 25), although the nature of these rights and the definition of who is covered by this section of the Act are not spelled out. The Meech Lake Accord and then the Charlottetown Accord—attempts at constitutional reform—proposed self-government for First Nations, but as we saw in chapter 3, both accords were defeated. A guarantee of the right to self-government—a major aim of First Nations —has still to be won.

Settling land claims is seen by many First Nations people as a way to gain some independence from the federal government, benefit from the resources of the land, and thus make some social and economic gains. The ability to make decisions at the band level, free of federal interference, is an important prerequisite to this independence. This does not mean that First Nations want to separate from Canada, but that they seek a new relationship with government that allows them to pursue their interests. Several local, regional, and national First Nations associations have been created to lobby for aboriginal rights and to pursue the resolution of land and treaty claims. At the national level, the Assembly of First Nations is the most important organization. Some progress has been made, but much remains to be done for First Nations bands across Canada to achieve political, economic, social, and cultural independence.[20]

First Nations Government

The federal government recognizes First Nations government only at the band level, and the federal government defines what constitutes a band. The chief and band council make bylaws—called band council resolutions—for the community on a reserve.

Under the *Indian Act*, councils make decisions for the reserve in such areas as health, traffic, law and order, road and building construction and other local works, and so on. However, council resolutions may be denied by the federal government or negated by provincial laws. Enforcing resolutions is also difficult when there is no Native police force or other enforcement agency on a reserve.[21] For these and other reasons, the Assembly of First Nations and other aboriginal organizations have made aboriginal self-government their major goal.

SUMMARY

Representative and responsible government are two fundamental principles of parliamentary democracy. These concepts manifest themselves in the structure of the federal and provincial governments, with their executive, legislative, and judicial branches of authority. Municipal governments are much simpler, though they affect our everyday lives more directly. Through the electoral process, Canadians have an opportunity to choose the party, platform, and person they feel will best represent their needs in the Canadian federation.

At the federal and provincial levels, proposed laws are called bills. There are various categories of bills, and the successful passage of a bill into law depends mainly on who initiates it.

First Nations have a unique relationship with the federal government and in Canada's political structure, a relationship that has its roots in colonial history. Years of attempts to control aboriginal peoples, and thereby assimilate them into the non-aboriginal population, have contributed to high levels of poverty, unemployment, loss of cultural identity, and other socioeconomic problems among First Nations. For these and other reasons, First Nations are seeking greater autonomy from government control and entrenchment of the right to self-government in the Canadian constitution. We will be revisiting the topic of self-government in later chapters.

KEY TERMS

representative government	minority government
responsible government	executive branch (federal)
member of Parliament	Cabinet
party loyalty	Cabinet solidarity
majority government	legislative branch (federal)

triple E Senate

bill

government bill

private member's bill

private bill

judicial branch

executive branch (provincial)

legislative branch (provincial)

municipal council

bylaw

NOTES

1. *Canada Elections Act*, RSC 1985, c. E-2, as amended.

2. For more details, see Elections Canada, *Election Handbook for Candidates, Their Official Agents and Auditors*, available at http://www.elections.ca, under "Publications."

3. See Ontario, Ministry of Municipal Affairs, *Candidate's Guide: 2000 Municipal Elections* (Toronto: Queen's Printer for Ontario, 2000), 2–5.

4. *Constitution Act, 1982*, RSC 1985, app. 2, no. 44.

5. *Canadian Charter of Rights and Freedoms*, part I of the *Constitution Act, 1982*, RSC 1985, app. II, no. 44.

6. *Income Tax Act*, RSC 1985, c. 1 (5th Supp.), as amended.

7. Office of the Legislative Assembly of Ontario, "Parliamentary Process: The Making and Passing of Laws," available at http://www.ontla.on.ca/information/process.htm.

8. Department of Justice Canada, "Provincial Courts," available at http://canada.justice.gc.ca/en/dept/pub/trib/PC.html#tp.

9. *Municipal Act*, RSO 1990, c. M.45.

10. Pam Williamson, *First Nations Peoples* (Toronto: Emond Montgomery, 1999), 142.

11. Assembly of First Nations Brotherhood (1999), http://www.afn.ca, quoted in Williamson, 142.

12. Williamson, 89–90.

13. *Indian Act*, RSC 1985, c. I-5, as amended.

14. Williamson, 128–29.

15. Max J. Hedley, "Native Peoples in Canada," in Kenneth G. Pryke and Walter C. Soderlund, eds., *Profiles of Canada* (Toronto: Copp Clark Pitman, 1992), 78.

16. Williamson, 91–99.

17. Williamson, 99–103; Hedley, 75–77.

18. Williamson, 178, 188, 193.

19. Hedley, 79.

20. Williamson, 146–48; Hedley, 76.

21. Williamson, 141–45.

EXERCISES

■ MULTIPLE CHOICE

1. The structure and role of government can be divided into three major functions:

    a. to be elected, to carry out election promises, and to represent citizens

    b. to enforce the rule of law, to authorize government actions, and to give legal authority to those actions

    c. to uphold constitutional rights, to pass new laws, and to administer public services

    d. to govern, to make laws, and to enforce those laws

    e. to represent citizens, to make laws, and to hold elections

2. Canada's head of state is

    a. the governor general

    b. the Queen

    c. the prime minister

    d. the lieutenant governor

    e. the Senate

3. The judiciary exists to

    a. make laws

    b. uphold the legitimacy of government

    c. legitimize the law

    d. make constitutional amendments

    e. enforce the principle of the rule of law

4. Key political decisions are made by

   a. the prime minister or premier and Cabinet

   b. political parties

   c. the Senate

   d. the governor general

   e. the Queen

5. A majority government is formed when

   a. one party has more MPs in the House of Commons than any other party

   b. one party's MPs hold a majority of seats in the House of Commons

   c. the Official Opposition has a majority of MPs in the House of Commons

   d. the majority of MPs are backbenchers

   e. the majority of MPs are appointed to Cabinet

■ TRUE OR FALSE?

_____ 1. If a political party does not win at least 151 seats in the House of Commons in an election, it automatically loses.

_____ 2. Cabinet solidarity refers to the principle of government members agreeing, at least publicly, on given policy matters.

_____ 3. Under the constitution, local governments are responsible for such services as roads, police, firefighting, sewers, water, garbage collection, and so on.

_____ 4. The _Indian Act_ and individual treaties govern the relationship between the federal government and First Nations.

_____ 5. Settling land claims is an important step toward aboriginal self-government since this would give some First Nations economic gains and, ultimately, make them less dependent on the federal government.

■ **SHORT ANSWER**

1. Define "responsible" government. How does it differ from "representative" government?

2. One criticism of Canada's political system is that far too much power is vested in the prime minister and Cabinet. What reforms might solve this problem?

3. What factors do you believe the prime minister should consider when choosing Cabinet ministers? What external factors might limit his or her choices?

4. Why has the Senate lost its credibility as an institution? What can be done to repair this image problem?

5. Why are First Nations seeking the right to self-government?

6. How do minority governments different from majority governments? Which do you prefer, and why?

CHAPTER 5

Politics, Society, and Law Enforcement

CHAPTER OBJECTIVES

After completing this chapter, you should be able to:

◆ Describe how the three levels of government cooperate in law enforcement.

◆ Relate the evolution of public law enforcement in Canada to broader socioeconomic changes in Canadian society.

◆ Relate the political spectrum model to the major federal political parties.

◆ Describe the major characteristics of Canadian political culture.

◆ Demonstrate how political ideology informs the development of public policy.

◆ Describe some of the major issues currently facing the justice system.

◆ Use information in this chapter to forecast future trends for law enforcement in Canada.

INTRODUCTION

Previous chapters have described how government structure and the political process have evolved in Canada and what this means in terms of the roles of the federal, provincial, and municipal governments. In this chapter we will see how these roles often overlap and affect one another in the area of law enforcement. We will then look at political and socioeconomic influences on law enforcement and the Canadian justice system. As we will discover, historical changes reveal much about current attitudes toward politics and the justice system.

Government activity should properly be viewed as organic in nature. It is a network where decisions in one area have consequences in another. Therefore, as you read, remain aware of these relationships. This will help you to put what you have studied into perspective.

GOVERNMENT RELATIONS

Recall from chapter 2 that the Fathers of Confederation anticipated a dominant role for the federal government, granting it blanket power over "peace, order and good government" and the ability to legislate in any areas not specifically mentioned in the constitution. The provinces were handed what were then considered to be minor areas of responsibility, such as education, health, and welfare. These were considered of little importance because at the time government usually did not fund or actively participate in running social programs. Instead, supporting these areas was considered the responsibility of the individual, family, or local community in the form of private charities and philanthropists. Increasing urbanization and industrialization after the turn of the twentieth century and growing public expectations have subsequently enhanced the significance of these provincial areas. The federal and provincial governments are regularly at odds over which has jurisdiction in a particular area, and these increasing squabbles over political turf have come to characterize Canada's political culture.

Ironically, municipal governments are the weakest politically of the three levels of government, even though the public services they provide affect us more directly on a daily basis than either of the other two government levels. Further, even though municipal politics provides the greatest opportunity for citizen participation in government, it attracts little public notice most of the time.

The constitution provides for the coordination of law enforcement across Canada. The federal government is responsible for creating criminal law, while the provinces are responsible for administering and enforcing its provisions and for creating and administering civil law. Municipal policing services are an extension of this provincial authority. Disagreements over how to approach justice issues can put provincial initiatives at odds with federal ones; similarly, local initiatives can be at odds with provincial ones. The remainder of this chapter will examine some of the political, social, economic, and other influences on law enforcement.

Evolution of Government Services

As Canada moved into the twentieth century and cities drew increasing numbers of people to industrial employment, the need for coordinated social services became acute. Existing private agencies lacked the resources and expertise necessary to meet the needs of urban-industrial society, and reformers began calling for government intervention in social services. Education in Ontario had become free, universal, and compulsory in 1871, and by the 1920s public health and social assistance were being regulated. The economic growth of Canada and the shift of the population to urban centres that began in the 1920s were factors that led the provincial governments to assert themselves more. Provincial concerns about federal domination have existed ever since.

Public demand for government-funded social services considerably enhanced provincial authority in the federal system, since the vast majority of these areas fell within their constitutional jurisdiction. However, limited provincial taxing capacity made it difficult to fund the ever-increasing costs of providing these services. Matters grew worse during the Great Depression of the 1930s as unemployment and poverty dramatically increased and federal funds were necessary to meet the added costs of running relief programs. This set the stage for the later pattern of **cost sharing**, where the federal government "topped up" provincial programs in return for setting national standards in that area. During and after World War II, the federal government continued to dominate provincial actions by using its **federal spending power** to fund programs in areas outside its constitutional jurisdiction. Taken together, these events had the effect of centralizing power at the federal level, since the provinces subsequently became dependent on federal money for social program funding.

cost sharing
funding of provincial programs that combines federal contributions with provincial funding

federal spending power
the power of the federal government to raise the greatest share of tax revenues

In the 1960s, the provinces began to reassert themselves in the Canadian federation, increasingly challenging Ottawa's dominant position. Beginning with Quebec's Quiet Revolution and spreading to other regions such as the West during the 1970s and 1980s, this more confrontational approach to federal–provincial relations has characterized Canadian politics up to the present day. Federal belt-tightening measures have aggravated the problem. As Ottawa has reduced its funding for social programs, provinces have called for more flexibility in the manner and means by which they deliver these services. Similarly, provincial government reductions in transfers to municipal governments have caused municipalities to either cut services or find new ways to fund them. In some communities, cost cutting has affected the quality of recreation programs, public maintenance, and emergency services as local politicians struggle to control costs while maintaining public services.

Law Enforcement at the Three Levels of Government

As Canada grew and moved toward a more urban and industrial way of life, new social realities and subsequent public concerns spawned changes in the nature and operation of policing within the justice system.

Public law enforcement, although jointly overseen by the federal justice and solicitor general departments and provincial attorneys and solicitors general, was for the most part left to individual communities to administer. The larger urban centres, such as Toronto and Montreal, were exceptions to the rule with their formal law enforcement systems. What has resulted from the constitutional division of powers is a sometimes confusing mix: the federal government creates laws governing the behaviour and activities of people and businesses; the provincial governments administer and enforce these laws, with some exceptions, through provincial agencies; and the municipal governments also enforce these laws through local police services, licensing, and so on.

The three levels of government often cooperate to safeguard the public safety of all Canadians. This cooperation provides for consistency and equity in enforcing the laws of Canada, especially in terms of criminal offences. The federal enforcement agencies, described below, work in concert with the various provincial and municipal enforcement services in combined forces operations, a prime example of the three levels of government working together for the public good and sharing costs.

Governments determine the kinds of laws we have and to what degree they are enforced. Also, each level of government except the municipal level is permitted by the constitution to raise sufficient funds through taxes to pay for the cost of operating various programs and services. By provincial law, municipal governments can raise money through property taxes.

The same applies to the administration of justice in the provinces. Again, by sharing in the operating costs, the federal government can greatly influence how justice is administered. Presently, Supreme Court of Canada justices are appointed and paid for by the federal government; lower-court judges are appointed and paid for by the provinces. Other differences in the justice system exist in the areas of correctional services for adult and young offenders, and in public policy and protection relative to combatting organized crime, among others.

Federal Law Enforcement

Accompanying economic and social changes was a gradual recognition of the importance of public policing to control crime and maintain civil order amid the transitions that were taking place in Canadian society. In 1873, Prime Minister John A. Macdonald, who was doing double duty as justice minister, supervised plans for a national police force "to bring law, order and Canadian authority to the North-West Territories (present-day Alberta and Saskatchewan)."[1] In doing so, Macdonald hoped to guard against American encroachment, maintain friendly relations with the First Nations peoples, and facilitate an orderly settlement of the region. Known initially as the Northwest Mounted Police (NWMP), this national police force was renamed the Royal Canadian Mounted Police (RCMP) in 1920.

During World Wars I and II, the NWMP/RCMP conducted border patrols and surveillance of potential security threats. In 1932, it consolidated a number of other government services to form the Marine Section to give Canada a national presence in its territorial waters. The RCMP also helped to create and coordinate a national database providing resources such as fingerprints, a crime index, firearms registration information, a photo section, and forensic expertise to help police investigators across the country. Potential internal security threats, exemplified by the FLQ Crisis of 1970 in Quebec (in which radical Quebec separatists kidnapped British diplomat James Cross and Quebec MNA Pierre Laporte and later killed Laporte), led to an expansion of security and intelligence operations, although these were formally separated from direct RCMP operations in 1984 with the creation of the Canadian Security and Intelligence Service (CSIS). Today, the RCMP has policing responsibilities in every province and territory, including policing contracts in eight provinces, three territories, and hundreds of municipalities.[2] The RCMP is administered by the federal Department of the Solicitor General.

Other enforcement agencies organized and paid for by the federal government include the Canada Customs and Revenue Agency, Immigration Canada, the Canadian Fisheries Agency, and the Canadian Coast Guard, which are administered by the appropriate ministries responsible for the area of jurisdiction. These agencies generally focus their efforts on their respective related federal laws, such as the *Customs Act*,[3] the *Excise Act*,[4] the *Immigration Act*,[5] the federal *Fisheries Act*,[6] and so on. Recently, the duties of Canada Customs officers have been extended to include enforcing *Criminal Code*[7] driving offences and other federal acts. Along with other federal enforcement officials, customs officers have been given the powers and protection of peace officers as described in the *Criminal Code*.

It is clear that the policies developed by the federal government greatly influence the kinds of services provided by the provincial governments. Historically, the federal government, because it collects the majority of tax money, determines the amount of money to transfer to each province for specific purposes. The lion's share is for social programs, particularly in the areas of health care and education, both provincial responsibilities. The amount of money transferred to the provinces generally depends on the provincial government following the wishes of the federal government, which is often led by a different political party from the provincial government.

Provincial Law Enforcement

Ontario and Quebec each has its own provincial police service that is administered in Ontario through the provincial Ministry of the Solicitor General. Provincial police work through joint forces operations with the RCMP and municipal police services to ensure that major criminal activities such as drug trafficking, illegal immigration, and counterfeiting are investigated efficiently and cost-effectively.

The history of provincial policing in Ontario dates back to 1875, when the first full-time paid criminal detective was hired by the attorney general's office. The staff gradually increased, and in 1909 an order-in-council was passed in the provincial legislature officially creating the Ontario Provincial Police (OPP) force.[8]

The history of the OPP reflects many similar historical themes to those of the RCMP, most notably in the areas of professionalization and technological innovation. Pioneers in highway patrol, OPP officers used motorcycles, marked cruisers, and after 1947, radio communication to enforce the province's *Highway Traffic Act*.[9] In fact, by 1956, 75 percent of provincial policing was taken up by this activity.[10] As with other government services, the OPP expanded greatly during the 1960s and 1970s. As we will see in coming chapters, the postwar period in Canada was a time of expansion in government services, including law enforcement. Police forces were able to keep up with technological changes as they emerged, and governments at all levels seemed ready, willing, and able to underwrite the additional costs. For example, this philosophy enabled the OPP to become the first force in North America to enforce traffic regulations from the air.[11]

Provincial governments seem to be intervening more and more in existing federal laws and policies. The federal *Young Offenders Act*,[12] for example, has been widely criticized since its inception in 1984, causing the proposed Youth Criminal Justice Act (Bill C-3) to be introduced.[13] When passed, young people who commit very serious criminal acts will likely be tried as adults, and parents of young offenders will be held more responsible for their children's behaviour. The Ontario provincial government recently passed the *Parental Responsibility Act*,[14] which imposes a fine of up to $6,000 on parents to pay for property damage or loss caused by children under 18, unless the parents can prove that the damage or loss was not intentional or that they provided reasonable supervision of their children.

Municipal Law Enforcement

police services board
civilian board that oversees a local police service

Municipal police services are administered by their **police services boards**, which consist of locally elected and appointed civilians. The board oversees the police service and establishes policies for managing the service, creates guidelines for dealing with public complaints against the police, approves operating budgets, and so on. It does not, however, deal with the day-to-day management of the police, which is done by the police service itself. A board can have as few as three members or as many as seven, depending on the size of the municipality.

INFLUENCES ON LAW ENFORCEMENT

Political Parties and the Political Spectrum

right-wing
a political attitude or philosophy that favours more individual freedom and less government intervention

left-wing
a political attitude or philosophy that favours more government intervention to help achieve social equality

political spectrum
a model that shows political philosophy on a continuum from left to right wing

Do you think, like many people, that the only thing distinguishing one political party from another is its name? While some parties do share similar platforms, many observers use the terms **right-wing** or **left-wing** to describe a party's fundamental philosophy. These terms have their origins in France, after the revolution of 1789, when the new political assembly was shaped like a semicircle. Members who favoured the traditional social hierarchy and economic status quo sat on the right side, while those who supported social equality and the major economic changes this would necessitate sat on the left. Moderate members—ones who favoured a more balanced approach to government—sat in the middle. Over the years, these labels have been attached to broader political ideas, which can be portrayed in a linear model called the **political spectrum** (see figure 5.1).

Today, "right" and "left" are generally associated with degrees of government involvement in the lives of citizens. Supporters of the right

■ **Figure 5.1   The Political Spectrum**

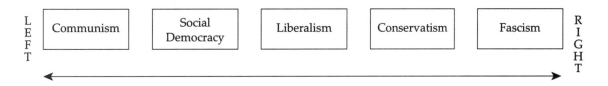

tend to prefer more individual freedom and less government intervention, particularly in the economy. This group thus supports measures such as the privatization of government-owned corporations and less government regulation of business in general. Those on the extreme right—also known as neoconservatism—favour policies such as tax cuts, less social spending, and more emphasis on individual responsibility. This group also tends to support "law and order" agendas, including tougher law enforcement and stiffer penalties for convicted criminals, a topic we will return to in the next section. Those on the left favour more government intervention, particularly in economic matters, with the aim of achieving greater social equality of citizens and mitigating the effects of an unpredictable economy.

Figure 5.2 is a diagram of where Canada's major federal political parties sit in relation to one another on the domestic political spectrum (the Bloc québécois, because of its philosophy based on French ethnicity and nationalism, does not easily fit into this model but tends to lean toward the left). On the international political spectrum, Canada is considered to be slightly left of centre in relation to the rest of the world, although recent policies of the Liberal government—for example, the downsizing of the federal public service during most of the 1990s, and Finance Minister Paul Martin's 2000 federal budget, which announced significant tax cuts—suggest we are moving further to the right.[15]

Political Parties and the History of Canada

Since Confederation, Canadians have witnessed the rise and fall of the major federal political parties. A historical context not only enables us to recognize some of the political, social, and economic factors that led to their creation, but also helps to explain why some parties have shifted their position on the political spectrum.

■ **Figure 5.2   Canadian Parties on the Political Spectrum**

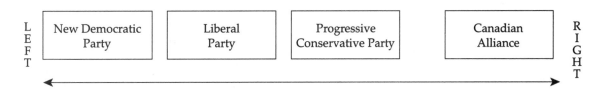

Only two parties have ever formed the federal government: the Progressive Conservative Party and the Liberal Party. Until almost the turn of the 20th century, federal politics was dominated by the Conservatives, created and guided by Sir John A. Macdonald, Canada's first prime minister. Under his tutelage, the party took a pro-business attitude, combining an allegiance to Britain with a deep mistrust of the United States.

Conversely, the Liberals dominated Canadian federal politics during most of the 20th century, having held power for almost 70 of those years.[16] Although it too had its beginnings around Confederation, the Liberal Party did not really come into its own until Wilfrid Laurier assumed its leadership in 1887. Unlike the Conservatives, the Liberals were more open to relations with the United States and had a strong base of support in Quebec.

Aside from a smattering of protest parties, these two parties dominated the political landscape during Canada's first 60 years. English–French relations proved to be a sore point for both parties during this time. Episodes such as the execution of Louis Riel in 1885, the Manitoba Schools Question in the early 1890s (over the replacement of a dual Protestant–Catholic school system in Manitoba with a single Protestant one), and the Conscription Crisis of World War I created deep divisions between French and English Canada, and neither party seemed able to address this problem to the satisfaction of the other side. The Great Depression of the 1930s, however, temporarily shifted the political focus away from French–English tensions.

During the Great Depression, many people became frustrated with the inability of the established parties to deal with the economic hardships. This eventually led to the creation of a new party in 1933—the Cooperative Commonwealth Federation. This decidedly left-wing party evolved into the New Democratic Party in the early 1960s, and although it has never formed a federal government, many of the social policies it supported were adopted by governing parties (the Canada Pension Plan and universal health care, for example).

After World War II, many Western countries instituted social programs in health care, education, and social assistance. In Canada, the growth of social welfare was due to many factors: a widespread fear of the economy sinking to Depression-level depths again after the war, labour shortages during the war that helped labour unions become more powerful, and a booming wartime economy that could afford to institute more government services were only some of the reasons. This shift to the left of the political spectrum lasted until the 1970s, when the political winds of conservatism began to reappear. Once more, the slow reaction of the existing political parties to this change proved to be the catalyst for the creation in 1987 of the Reform Party, which changed its name in the spring of 2000 to the Canadian Alliance. Created as a party supporting Western Canadian concerns, the Alliance espouses right-wing policies such as cuts to taxes, cuts to social programs, smaller government, and stricter controls on immigration.

As with their adoption of NDP policies in the 1960s, the federal Liberals have been able to capitalize on the general shift to the political right by borrowing many of the Alliance's policies and presenting them in a more moderate form. This has allowed the party to appeal to right-wing voters and maintain its existing support. The Liberals have also been fortunate that resurgent Quebec nationalism, illustrated by the rise of the Bloc québécois in federal politics, now appears to be on the decline. All in all, one can argue that the reason the Liberal Party has been so successful is because it has been able to strike the proper balance between harsh political ideology and the current mood of the country.

Law Enforcement and the Political Spectrum

"Tough on crime." "Law and order candidate." "Victims' rights."

Perhaps you have noticed such slogans and similar ones during recent political campaigns in your community. Where do they come from, and what informs their message? Most of us would agree that criminal behaviour in Canadian society is indeed a bad thing and every attempt should be made to prevent crime and preserve civil order. How a government chooses to go about these tasks reveals a lot about its ideological preferences.

The moral viewpoints of the political party in power have always had a major impact on the kinds of government services provided to Canadians. Each political party has its own views on how Canada should be managed and which government services should be given priority, including those that apply to public safety. For example, federal corrections is moving away from mega-jails and toward smaller institutions and rehabilitation, while provinces such as Ontario have shut down smaller jails, opting for private mega-jails and a "get-tough" approach, particularly in the area of young offenders. These different philosophies reflect ideological disagreements over how to deal with crime in society. These become clear when we look at where each political party in power sits on the political spectrum.

Right-wing ideology tends to emphasize self-reliance, individual responsibility, and a "survival of the fittest" attitude toward society. Therefore, issues of crime and punishment focus on making individuals accountable for the choices they have made—that is, "Do the crime, do the time." On the other hand, left-wing ideology emphasizes collective responsibility and sees the state as a means through which to overcome inequality and look after those who are unable to look after themselves. Thus, left-wing proponents see criminals as products of a social system that prevents them from achieving their potential. In the eyes of the left, "It's the system that's at fault."

Should governments spend more money on hunting, prosecuting, and incarcerating criminals, or should it focus on resolving the social conditions that lead to criminal acts? Left-wing ideology emphasizes the social problems, institutions, and policies that create an environment for crime. For example, it currently costs Canadian taxpayers $9.5 billion to operate the criminal justice system. The cost to keep someone in a federal prison is approximately $46,000 per year, and almost double that amount to keep a young offender in secure custody. On the other hand, research shows that for every $1 governments invest in social programs that help young children, they will save $7 in the costs of crime, welfare, and educational upgrading.[17]

There is no right or wrong answer here; rather, it is a question of resource allocation. Crime will always be a part of society. The question we as citizens should consider is what is the most efficient and effective way to mitigate crime and its consequences?

Canadian Political Culture

political culture
the basic attitudes people have toward each other, the state, and authority

Political culture refers to "the basic attitudes people have toward each other, the state and authority, that in essence reflect the impact of history on a society's beliefs."[18] Canadian political culture has been and continues to be influenced by a number of factors. Our political views have been shaped by our history and geography and by the diversity of our population.

Canada evolved from former French and British colonies, all of which were carved from lands once occupied by First Nations peoples. The mutual agreement and cooperation necessary for Confederation and coexistence between these two dominant linguistic groups have infused Canadian politics with a tendency for compromise, rather than confrontation, when disagreements appear.

Regionalism

Regional loyalties have always coloured the Canadian political landscape. Within our immense geography are several regions—notably, the West, Atlantic Canada, British Columbia, Ontario, Quebec, and Newfoundland —all with differing interests and viewpoints as to how the Canadian political system can and should function. These feelings have even manifested themselves through the formation of formal political parties, such as Reform in the Western provinces, and the Parti québécois and Bloc québécois in Quebec.

Regionalism has been strengthened by economic disparity, some of which dates back to the time of Confederation. For example, the residents of such regions as the North, the Atlantic provinces (particularly Newfoundland), and the predominantly agricultural Prairie provinces such as Saskatchewan face limited opportunities due to an inhospitable climate, a lack of development, diminishing natural resources, and so on. Canadians have thus tended to relocate to areas that promise better opportunities, creating large urban centres whose residents have high expectations of the better life. The majority of immigrants also tend to settle in the major urban centres, where jobs and housing, schools and other facilities are more plentiful. This concentration in a few major cities poses many challenges and creates social problems, not the least of which is a growing gap between the "haves" and the "have nots." We see this shift occurring in the lower mainland of British Columbia, in the large cities of Alberta, and also in Southern Ontario, which is experiencing a dramatic growth in population. These regions tend to have low unemployment and a high cost of living. They also tend to have growing numbers of homeless people, higher crime rates, and other social problems.

US Influence

Our geographic proximity to the United States also informs our Canadian identity. The overwhelming barrage of American culture and the United States' close economic relations with Canada have blurred traditional differences between what is considered cultural preservation and what is considered economic protectionism. For example, after hearing a case brought to it by the United States, the World Trade Organization ruled in 1997 that Canadian laws aimed at protecting the Canadian magazine industry from American competition in the form of split-run magazines (US magazines that publish a Canadian edition) violated international trading rules.

Multiculturalism

Canada's political culture has also developed out of a long tradition of immigration from the arrival of the First Nations to today. Our constitution recognizes two dominant European cultures—French and English—and confirms that Canada has two official languages. Although English–French conflict still exercises considerable influence on Canadian politics, aboriginal voices, as well as those of many more cultures and communities, add new flavours to the political mix.

Traditional politics has also been influenced tremendously by the *Charter of Rights and Freedoms*,[19] which enshrines **multiculturalism** as a characteristic of Canadian society that is to be maintained and enhanced. The Charter has permitted citizens and individuals to participate in political decision making through the courts, forcing politicians to recognize constitutional guarantees in policy matters. Some critics have charged that this change has removed the spirit of compromise that characterized the politics of earlier times.[20] This debate demonstrates the ongoing evolution of political culture in Canada, and serves to remind us that although political culture is informed by past events, it cannot be held prisoner by them forever.

multiculturalism
cultural and racial diversity; in Canada, a constitutionally enshrined policy that recognizes the diversity of our population

Canada's multiculturalism policy aims to promote the full participation of *all* Canadians in our society, tolerance for diversity, and a reduction in prejudice. This policy applies to everyone, not just to recent immigrants or particular ethnic groups. Note, however, that many First Nations members are not in favour of being lumped under multicultural policies (as they are in the Charter) because of the unique problems they face that are a result of a history of colonization.[21]

First Nations

Chapter 4 introduced some of the history of First Nations' relations with government, including some of the reasons for increased aboriginal activism and desire for self-government. In the last decade Canadians have witnessed some serious confrontations between First Nations bands and law enforcement agents over land claims, traditional hunting and fishing rights, logging rights, and other issues. The events in Oka, Quebec and Burnt Church, New Brunswick are only two examples.

It is important to remember that although we use the term "First Nations" for convenience, this term encompasses many groups, who are characterized by historical and contemporary diversity. The Inuit people of the Far North, for example, have a very different lifestyle and cultural traditions from the Plains Indians bands. Even today, with the growing aboriginal movement to address the social, economic, and other ills that have characterized the lives of many bands since colonial times, there are widely differing views on how to achieve these aims, including whether civil disobedience is justified to make their voices heard.

aboriginal self-government
greater autonomy of First Nations to pursue their own political, social, cultural, and economic objectives with limited interference from the federal government

A substantial shift of responsibility for First Nations, including the administration of reserves and of government-funded services to reserves, is occurring as more and more bands successfully win the right to **self-government**. We have witnessed this in Western Canada in the settling of large land claims and in the creation of First Nations police services on some reserves (for example, the Dakota-Ojibway Police Service of Brandon, Manitoba). More recently, the mostly Inuit Nunavut Territory is planning not only its own police service but also self-managed courts and correctional services. These are truly historic steps in the First Nations fight for self-determination, but we must keep in mind that these steps do not solve the serious problems—low life expectancy, lack of basic infrastructure and government services, high unemployment, and low education levels, to name only a few—faced by aboriginal peoples.

What exactly does aboriginal self-government mean? Basically, it means bands are allowed to pursue their own policies rather than government-imposed ones. Instead of reserves being simply places set aside by government for the purpose of controlling people, the reserves become communities that develop economic activities, services, infrastructure, and so on for the benefit of their residents—just like any other community in Canada. However, note that overall control of reserve policy is still in the hands of the federal government as set down in the constitution. The right to self-government has yet to be added to the constitution (although First Nations groups have been fighting for such an amendment for years). Despite obstacles, some of which go back almost 400 years, First Nations continue to strive for greater political, economic, social, and cultural independence.[22]

In practical terms, self-government will have effects on law enforcement and the justice system. Some of the changes already include aboriginal police services (see below), which have been replacing the RCMP and OPP on reserves. Efforts are being made to recruit more people of aboriginal descent as court workers, paralegals, justices of the peace, legal clinic staff, and so on. These measures are intended to bring elements of First Nations culture and custom to the justice system and make it more responsive to the needs of First Nations offenders. A very new form of alternative justice is the sentencing circle, made up of community members, that has been set up on some reserves. Sentencing circles hear cases involving First Nations offenders that are believed appropriate to remove from the court system and addressed at the community level. The circle may impose a sentence that includes community service, counselling, or restitution to the victim in some form.[23]

FIRST NATIONS POLICING   First Nations policing is a relatively recent innovation in public law enforcement. It has evolved out of a desire on the part of aboriginal communities to police themselves and a growing public understanding of the need for and benefits of policing that recognizes the unique traits of the many aboriginal cultures. Beginning in the 1970s as a series of joint pilot projects, aboriginal policing has developed into a complex system of operations that can involve individual communities, and the federal and provincial levels of government.

In 1991, the federal government passed legislation setting up the legal and bureaucratic framework for self-policing in aboriginal communities across Canada. In 2000, 127 agreements were in place across Canada to facilitate these police services. The variety of treaties and diversity of communities defy absolute bureaucratic standardization; however, there are some general principles upon which all policing agreements are based. First, because aboriginal relations fall within federal jurisdiction, it is ultimately the responsibility of the federal solicitor general to work with aboriginal communities to set up and manage policing services in each community. However, in many instances, provincial governments assist in funding, training, and administration.

Increasingly, First Nations police services are developing into organizations similar in structure and authority to those in non-aboriginal areas. In northern Ontario, for example, the Nishnawbe-Aski Police Service is regarded as a regional service similar to those of York, Peel, and South Simcoe–West Gwillimbury police services. Although not subject to the provincial *Police Services Act*, the force trains its recruits at the Ontario Police College. Fifty-two percent of Nishnawbe-Aski's funding comes from the federal government, while the Ontario government makes up the remainder. In 2000, its budget totalled $11 million. The Nishnawbe-Aski Police Service currently employs 97 officers and 25 civilian staff.[24]

Special Interest Groups and Citizens' Organizations

In Canada, social movements have tended to be based around "region, workplace, and household."[25] For example, French nationalism (and the desire for Quebec separation) is probably the most significant regional movement in Canada. Other important movements include the labour (union) movement, environmentalism, multiculturalism, the women's movement, and the gay and lesbian rights movement. In recent years, the effects of globalism—the interrelationships among cultures and economies around the world—have been gaining momentum. Important political decisions cannot be made without considering their effects on others.

In a democratic state, politicians are supposed to consider all points of view, but there remains the danger that when some voices become too loud they drown out other voices or cause them to be ignored altogether. Organizations such as Mothers Against Drunk Driving (MADD) and victims' rights groups have become much more active in lobbying public officials in order to have their views reflected in legislation. As we have seen throughout the first half of this text, Canada owes much of its enviable quality of life to its tradition of consultation and compromise.

Government Downsizing and Public Opinion

We pay various forms of taxes to the three levels of governments to pay for the services they provide. Federal and provincial income taxes are based on the income earned by individuals and businesses. Other taxes include the federal goods and services tax (GST), provincial sales tax (PST) in all provinces except Alberta, and local property taxes based on an assessment of the property municipal residents own, which is generally determined by the market value. Governments also raise revenue by assessing fees for various licences and permits, including business, vehicle, hunting, fishing, and firearms licences, among others. As well, special programs such as employment insurance and Canada Pension Plan are funded by employer–employee payroll deductions.

It seemed in past years that the cost of operating government programs was of no concern and that the money necessary to pay for them was easily attainable. Only in recent years have Canadians begun to realize just how indebted they are due to government spending and have governments begun to balance their budgets. Interestingly, municipal governments, by provincial law, cannot run deficits (spend more than they collect in taxes)—they establish a working budget and then assess the cost against the local ratepayers (taxpayers).

As government deficits ballooned in the 1970s and 1980s, public concern over government waste and inefficiency forced public officials to rethink the role of the state in citizens' lives, ushering in a decade of cutbacks and downsizing in government services in the 1990s. Policing in Canada has not been immune from these government initiatives to save money. Police budgets are now coming under much more scrutiny than in the past, while police forces are expected to maintain service and adapt to increasingly sophisticated criminal activities. The threats of organized crime and Internet fraud require cutting-edge computer technology and surveillance equipment—expensive propositions for cash-strapped agencies. As an example, in planning its 2000 budget, the City of Toronto told all of its departments to cut spending by 5 percent. But its police force said it would need a 10 percent increase in its budget just to maintain its current level of service (the request was made on the justification that the department had to pay officers overtime for off-duty court appearances and to keep up with inflation).[26]

The issue of "blank cheque" funding for police services is often justified with the adage "Crime doesn't take holidays." While this is no doubt true, we as citizens have to remember that it is our tax dollars that pay for policing and other services, and bigger budgets in the public sector present politicians with the dilemma of either cutting service in other areas or raising taxes to cover the additional cost.

At the same time, reductions in the number of criminal offences in Canada have caused some politicians to question the need for increased police budgets. Recently released statistics show that Canada's overall crime rate has been declining for eight years, with 1999 representing the lowest rate in two decades.[27] However, as experts point out, this trend may be due to Canada's aging population and the current economic boom. Statistically, crime rates tend to be higher in people aged 15 to 24, who now represent a relatively small percentage of Canada's population.[28]

Despite this data, concern for public safety and security have remained hot issues. Booming sales of alarm systems and anti-theft devices, as well as a marked growth in private security (for example, corporate and private security guards), all suggest that Canadians are feeling less, not more, safe. An aging workforce and budget restraints have led to chronic shortages of police officers, accelerated the growth of private law enforcement, and forced large police services to reorganize in an attempt to cut costs and improve efficiency. For example, the OPP has reconfigured its operations from 17 to 6 regions (encompassing 93 detachments) across the province, while the RCMP has created 4 regions and eliminated subdivisions, creating geographical districts. Despite recent hiring, past budget cuts have left the number of Toronto police officers almost 10 percent below what it was in 1992.[29] While cost savings and efficiency lie at the heart of these initiatives, it is still too early to assess whether they are achieving these goals.

POLICE RESPONSES TO A CHANGING SOCIETY

All of the influences discussed above have caused policing services to rethink and reorganize the way they do business, and to recruit personnel that mirror the people they serve. In addition, **community policing** has become commonplace all across Canada. Community policing is based on a belief that the officer on the street and members of the community can work together to prevent crime and resolve disputes. This approach emphasizes greater communication between police and residents, more input on local issues from rank-and-file officers and the public, an attempt to have the police force reflect the diversity of the surrounding community, and a more people-oriented approach to policing in general.[30]

community policing
approach to policing based on the police and the community working together

The Ontario *Police Services Act*[31] sets out six principles on which police services are based. Note how the spirit of community policing is contained in these principles.

1. Declaration of principles.—Police services shall be provided throughout Ontario in accordance with the following principles:

1. The need to ensure the safety and security of all persons and property in Ontario.

2. The importance of safeguarding the fundamental rights guaranteed by the *Canadian Charter of Rights and Freedoms* and the *Human Rights Code*.

3. The need for co-operation between the providers of police services and the communities they serve.

4. The importance of respect for victims of crime and understanding of their needs.

5. The need for sensitivity to the pluralistic, multiracial and multicultural character of Ontario Society.

6. The need to ensure that police forces are representative of the communities they serve.

Following these principles benefits police services as well as the community, because officers that reflect their community and behave in appropriate ways receive more respect and cooperation from the public. Also note that being representative of the community does not only mean in a multicultural sense, but also that police services should include more female officers.

Most citizens have a limited understanding of how different policing is in the 21st century from what it was a generation ago. It is no longer simply a matter of responding to crimes after they have occurred. Officers are involved in school and community-based programs to deter crime (for example, Crime Stoppers and Neighbourhood Watch) and victim assistance programs that provide support for victims of crime. In addition, police forces have made concerted efforts to be sensitive to, and representative of, the social and ethnic diversity of the citizens in their respective communities. In Toronto alone last year, police officers attended an estimated 3,000 meetings in order to make contacts with various groups.[32] Efforts are being made to actively recruit officers from historically underrepresented groups, including people of colour, women, and aboriginal peoples. Police forces in large urban centres are attempting to form positive links with community groups representing a wide range of interests in an effort to gain their support. In Toronto, for example, Chief of Police Julian Fantino has met repeatedly with members of the black and the gay and lesbian communities to solicit input and offer reassurance that their interests are not being ignored.[33]

In recent years, some police officers have expressed concern that politicians are out of touch with the reality of police work. Police want to have greater input and influence in political decisions that affect them. Politicians and members of the public have been slow to acknowledge the greatly increased workload now expected of individual officers. Groups such as the Canadian Association of Chiefs of Police, the Ontario Association of Chiefs of Police, the Ontario Provincial Police Association, and the Ontario Association of Police Officers are making their positions known on a variety of justice-related issues. Through these and other associations, the police are now taking a much more active role by publicly questioning political decisions. Some have even been accused of raising funds to support politicians who are friendly to their cause and to target those who are not. As will be discussed in chapter 8, critics charge that this greater political activism threatens the integrity of civilian authority over police and the fundamental principles of elected representation.

SUMMARY

Politics and history have had and continue to have a significant role in the development of public law enforcement in Canada. In the country's early years, law enforcement agencies, like other government departments, were limited in both scope and size due in large part to the sheer size of the country and the contemporary understanding of what constituted effective law enforcement.

As Canada transformed itself from a rural-agricultural into a more urban-industrial society, new realities and the resulting new demands imposed themselves on public law enforcement agencies. The arrival of mass communication, transportation networks, and technological innovations have both challenged and changed the justice system.

The political spectrum informs the ideologies of the major federal parties in Canada. Each government is influenced by the political and moral views of its elected body, and these views inform the analysis of, and proposed solutions to, social issues. This is especially true relative to policing services, crime, and the administration of justice. The three levels of government often have interrelated and overlapping roles and responsibilities, and we see this particularly in the area of law enforcement. This situation can be beneficial, as in the case of joint efforts to combat crime, but it can also result in government agencies working against, rather than with, one another.

Popular demand for greater government accountability and fiscal restraint have affected police services, resulting in reorganization and fresh dialogue with individuals and groups representing a variety of backgrounds, including First Nations and other cultural groups, citizens' organizations, and so on. Part of this new strategy is an attempt to communicate to the public how policing has changed over the years so that the communities being served better understand the realities of the job and the demands being placed on rank-and-file police officers.

KEY TERMS

cost sharing	political spectrum
federal spending power	multiculturalism
police services board	aboriginal self-government
right-wing	community policing
left-wing	

NOTES

1. RCMP, "Historical Highlights," available at http://www.rcmp-grc.gc.ca/html/history.htm.

2. RCMP, "Contract Policing Branch," available at http://www.rcmp-grc.gc.ca/html/contract.htm.

3. *Customs Act*, RSC 1985, c. 1 (2nd Supp.).

4. *Excise Act*, RSC 1985, c. E-12.

5. *Immigration Act*, RSC 1985, c. 1-2.

6. *Fisheries Act*, RSC 1985, c. F-27.

7. *Criminal Code*, RSC 1985, c. C-46, as amended.

8. OPP, "A Brief History of the Ontario Provincial Police," available at http://www.gov.on.ca/opp/museum/english/briefhistory.htm.

9. *Highway Traffic Act*, RSO 1990, c. H.8.

10. OPP, "A Brief History."

11. Ibid.

12. *Young Offenders Act*, RSC 1985, c. Y-1, as amended.

13. This bill died on the order paper when the federal government called an election in 2000, but was expected to be reintroduced.

14. *Parental Responsibility Act*, SO 2000, c. 4.

15. See William Walker, "Martin's Big Tax Return," *The Toronto Star* (February 29, 2000), A1; Stephen Thorne, "Public Servants Paying the Price for Job Cuts," *The Toronto Star* (April 22, 2000), A6.

16. The exceptions were 1911–21, 1930–35, 1957–63, 1979–80, and 1984–93. John Robert Colombo, ed., *1999 Canadian Global Almanac* (Toronto: Macmillan, 1998), 122–30 (based on information from Elections Canada).

17. Rob Tripp, "Dollars and Pain: The Economics of the Justice System," *Kingston Whig Standard* (November 25, 1996).

18. Charles Hauss and William Smith, *Comparative Politics—Domestic Responses to Global Challenges: A Canadian Perspective*, 3rd ed. (Scarborough: Nelson, 2000), 10.

19. *Canadian Charter of Rights and Freedoms*, part I of the *Constitution Act, 1982*, RSC 1985, app. II, no. 44.

20. Hauss and Smith, 63–64.

21. Shahé Kazarian, *Diversity Issues in Policing* (Toronto: Emond Montgomery, 1998), 22.

22. Max J. Hedley, "Native Peoples in Canada," in Kenneth G. Pryke and Walter C. Soderlund, *Profiles of Canada* (Toronto: Copp Clark Pitman, 1992), 88.

23. Pam Williamson, *First Nations Peoples* (Toronto: Emond Montgomery, 1999), 227–29.

24. The authors wish to thank Nishnawbe-Aski Police Service Chief of Police B.W. Luloff for research and support materials. Thanks also to Allan R. Morrison, Education Officer/Special Projects Coordinator, at Windigo First Nations Council.

25. Barry D. Adam, "Social Inequality in Canada," in Kenneth G. Pryke and Walter C. Soderlund, *Profiles of Canada* (Toronto: Copp Clark Pitman), 64.

26. See Jack Lakey, "Toronto Police Seeking $570 Million Budget," *The Toronto Star* (December 10, 1999), B3; Paul Moloney, "Police Can Trim $4.8 Million, Jakobek Says," *The Toronto Star* (February 28, 2000), B2; Bageshree Paradkar, "Court Duty, Protests, Add to Overtime," *The Toronto Star* (February 17, 2000), B3.

27. Elaine Carey, "GTA Leads Way as Crime Drops Across Canada," *The Toronto Star* (July 19, 2000), A1. Current statistics available at Statistics Canada online: http://www.statcan.ca/english/Pgdb/State/Justice/legal02.htm. See also "Crime and Justice" in Colombo, ed., *Canadian Global Almanac*, 189–93.

28. Carey, A1.

29. Julian Fantino, radio interview, *Here and Now*, CBC Radio One, July 19, 2000.

30. Kazarian, 8–9.

31. *Police Services Act*, RSO 1990, c. P.15, as amended.

32. Fantino, radio interview.

33. In Toronto, for example, Chief Julian Fantino has met repeatedly with members of the black, and gay and lesbian communities to solicit input and offer reassurance. See Bruce DeMara, "Fantino Faces Gay Critics," *The Toronto Star* (January 27, 2000), A3; Heather Greenwood, "Great Divide Over Policing Shrinks a Bit," *The Toronto Star* (June 25, 2000), A2.

EXERCISES

■ MULTIPLE CHOICE

1. Public law enforcement is administered by

    a. the federal government

    b. the provincial governments

    c. the municipal governments

    d. all three levels of government

    e. none of the above

2. "Political culture" refers to

    a. the attitudes of politicians about government

    b. basic attitudes of citizens toward each another, the government, and authority

    c. political views that have been shaped by a country's history and geography

    d. a and b

    e. b and c

3. "Left-wing" refers to

    a. a seat on the left side of the House of Commons

    b. a political philosophy that emphasizes tax cuts and smaller government

    c. a political philosophy that emphasizes social welfare and the collective good

    d. a political philosophy that emphasizes individualism and little government intervention

    e. all of the above

4. The following parties have formed the federal government since Confederation:

    a. New Democratic Party and Progressive Conservative Party

    b. Liberal Party and New Democratic Party

    c. Canadian Alliance and Progressive Conservative Party

    d. Conservative Party and Liberal Party

    e. New Democratic Party and Canadian Alliance

5. Right-wing ideologists tend to believe that

   a. criminals should go to prison

   b. crime is a product of inequalities in the social system

   c. criminals must take responsibility for their actions

   d. a and b

   e. a and c

■ TRUE OR FALSE?

____ 1. Municipal policing services are an extension of provincial authority over the administration and enforcement of criminal law.

____ 2. Through cost sharing, the federal government can greatly influence how justice is administered in the provinces.

____ 3. Someone who supports right-wing ideology tends to view crime as a product of a social system that is inherently unequal.

____ 4. Someone who supports left-wing ideology tends to view crime as an individual choice and therefore an individual responsibility.

____ 5. The close proximity of the United States has no effect on Canada's political culture.

■ SHORT ANSWER

1. Explain how the different levels of government work together to provide policing services.

2. How do social realities affect decisions about what policing services are provided at the federal, provincial, and local levels and the nature of these services?

3. What is aboriginal self-government? What is its purpose?

4. As a city councillor, how would you deal with proposed police budget increases? Explain your answer.

5. Outline the arguments for and against active police participation in the political process.

6. What do you believe is an appropriate role for interest groups in the political process? What are the risks of an imbalance in this participation?

7. How might the principles of cooperation and compromise be employed to overcome current disagreements over the role of police in the political process?

8. Which side of the political spectrum most appeals to you? Why?

9. Choose the federal party you believe you will support in the next election. On what basis do you make this choice? Visit the party's Web site and see whether it has any information on the subjects you are interested in.

10. Using the framework of the political spectrum, choose three news items and analyze them from a left-wing and a right-wing perspective. How are the solutions to these issues coloured by the respective ideologies?

PART III

Public Administration

CHAPTER 6

A Cog in the Machine: Public Administration and Bureaucracies

CHAPTER OBJECTIVES

After completing this chapter, you should be able to:

◆ Define public administration and describe its relation to the political process in Canada.

◆ Explain and compare theoretical concepts of bureaucracy.

◆ Outline the benefits and drawbacks of each concept.

◆ Describe the degree to which each of these concepts has been adopted by private and public bureaucracies.

◆ Outline the differences between public and private enterprise.

◆ Using examples, assess the benefits and drawbacks of privatizing the public sector.

INTRODUCTION

"Prime Minister Promises $1 Million to Each Canadian."

Hold on! Before you drop this text and run off in search of your share of the cash, think for a moment about where exactly you'd be searching for this windfall. The prime minister's residence probably wouldn't be high on your list. You might visit the local federal government building or phone a federal government office in an attempt to discover how to receive payment. Now the bad news—as far as the authors know, there is in fact no substance to this headline (but we could be wrong!). The good news is that, if you reacted to this headline as stated, you have already demonstrated an understanding of the difference between the political and administrative elements of government. Even though the prime minister announces that funding will be made available for all kinds of programs, the actual distribution of these funds or the services they provide is carried out by a vast and complex network of people and institutions referred to collectively as the public service.

Because of the close interaction between politics and public administration, it can be difficult to distinguish between them. Both are responsible for managing the day-to-day operation of government. Similarly, political and administrative bodies attempt to respond to citizens' needs by discussing and developing public policy. However, public administration differs from its political counterpart in several ways. First, we do not directly elect public servants. Instead, they are usually hired in much the same way as any other employee, although as we will see, some may be appointed by government to sit on a board or carry out a special duty. Second, public administration is ideally concerned with how to implement political will rather than with deciding what it is the public actually wants. Thus, in the above fantasy, it is the public service that would serve as the vehicle by which each of us would receive our money. In short, politicians make decisions while public servants implement, or carry out, those decisions.

THEORIES OF BUREAUCRACY

The model we have just described provides a general explanation of the relationship between politics and public administration, but this ongoing interaction is seldom this simple. The administrative side alone involves thousands of bureaucrats—basically, unelected government officials—intricate layers of communication, and an adherence to rules and regulations for the purposes of evaluation and accountability. This administrative machinery that supports government has been with us for as long as civilization itself. As humans began to congregate in larger and larger groups, structures of government developed; in turn, rulers depended on others to carry out their wishes. It is no surprise then that societies with highly developed bureaucracies were capable of considerable achievements.

bureaucracy
the organizational structure through which government exercises its power

bureaucrat
public servant

Though the word has many popular negative connotations, a **bureaucracy** is really just an organizational structure through which governments put their decisions into action. The word is a combination of the French *bureau*, for desk or office, and the Greek *cratie*, for rule. A **bureaucrat** is simply an employee of a bureaucracy—a public servant. Huge bureaucracies existed in ancient China and Egypt, societies whose legacy lives with us today in the Great Wall and the pyramids, respectively. Bureaucrats even had an effect on the location of Jesus's birth! Mary and Joseph went to Bethlehem in accordance with Roman policy, which decreed that people must return to their hometowns for taxation purposes. Thus, while they form an integral part of society, public bureaucracies have for the most part gone unnoticed or have been overshadowed by events with which most of us are familiar.

The nature and function of bureaucracies began to interest political thinkers during the 19th century. The field has expanded greatly since then, helped along by the theoretical ideas of several notable figures. These people can be categorized according to three general schools of thought: classic, structuralist, and human relations or humanist. We will deal with each category separately.

Classic Theories of Bureaucracy

Karl Marx (1818–1883)

Karl Marx is best known for developing the political ideology of communism. In general terms, this way of thinking about society proposed that **capitalism**[1] creates two classes of people: the poorer class, collectively known as the proletariat, and the wealthier class, which Marx called the bourgeoisie. Marx argued that this class division occurs because competition in the free market forces bourgeois employers to exploit their proletariat employees—that is, work them as hard as possible for as little money as possible. Marx observed the terrible working conditions spawned by the Industrial Revolution of the late 1700s through the mid-1800s. This was a time of major economic changes as new machinery and technology revolutionized industry. The mainly rural population of Europe and other parts of the world moved to the cities in greater and greater numbers in search of jobs in the new factories. A new—and poverty-stricken—working class developed that worked under sometimes appallingly dangerous conditions and Marx became convinced that it was just a matter of time before workers would overthrow these capitalist oppressors, creating a society with no social classes or private ownership.

capitalism
an economic system based on private ownership and competition in a free market

Marx speculated that eventually there would be no need for government because people would work toward a common good and share equally in resources. As far as Marx was concerned, government was nothing more than a tool of the wealthy classes that they used to maintain their positions of social and economic privilege. Bureaucracy was merely an extension of this apparatus, a means of legitimating state oppression of the working classes while perpetuating an illusion of fairness, justice, and objectivity. Marx reasoned that as workers collectively became aware of their situation, conflict would increase between workers and the dominant classes. The latter would respond by resorting to more violence to keep the lower classes in line. For instance, the police or army might be called upon to break up demonstrations or intervene in labour disputes. Thus, for Marx, the civil service was part of a systemic social problem of one class over another, and bureaucracy became more complex as government attempted to deal with class conflict.

Many scholars have attempted to interpret Marxist theory and explain its relevance to current events. Referred to as neo-Marxists, this group argues that the state exists for three major purposes. First, it accumulates and concentrates wealth and power within the wealthy classes. For example, the state may give the rich favourable tax treatment or provide corporations with generous job creation subsidies. Second, the state serves to legitimize the disadvantaged position of the working classes by pretending that social inequality is simply the result of the natural superiority of the upper classes. In other words, those on top deserve to be there by virtue of the fact that they are there. Finally, the state exists to quash any social unrest that may emerge as a result of worker dissatisfaction with the status quo.[2]

Criticism of Marxist Theory

One criticism of Marxist social analysis is that it cannot adequately explain the social mobility that takes place among members of different classes. For example, some people who are born into a disadvantaged class are able to work their way up to a higher class. Marxism also stereotypes people according to the class to which they belong and therefore cannot accommodate individual differences. In addition, notions of social class are difficult to define. Most Canadians like to think of themselves as middle class; however, the definition of what this actually means, even in terms of income, varies widely across the country.

Still, Marxist philosophy does provide some insights about how and why public bureaucracies function as they do, particularly when it comes to public law enforcement. Marxist analysis imbues a negative view of government, and this has implications for institutions that are charged with preserving public safety and civil order. It casts state armies and police forces as defenders of an unfair and self-serving regime, protecting and preserving the property and entitlements of the dominant classes. Thus, when workers attempt to force any changes on the existing social order, the upper classes can call on these law enforcement agencies to counter the perceived threat. They can also use other government institutions, such as the legal system, to deal with resistance. As a result, neo-Marxist theory puts little faith in the integrity of law enforcement, viewing it with suspicion and in need of constant monitoring.

Max Weber (1864–1920)

Max Weber was a German scholar who studied social issues using systematic methods. As we learned in the first chapter of this text, bureaucracies have existed for as long as human civilization; however, it was Weber who pioneered the study of bureaucratic structure, function, and behaviour. His work remains relevant today because it offers insights into the ways public policy is developed and acted on.

Weber began his study of bureaucracy by relating it to previous work he had done in the field of political sociology. He identified three sources of authority that can form the basic power structure in a society: traditional authority, charismatic authority, and legal authority. **Traditional authority** refers to the right of someone to rule because of his or her heredity, religion, or divine right (a right sanctioned by a higher spiritual power). A good example of this is provided by the British monarchy, which has claimed legitimacy to rule using all of these criteria at different periods in history. **Charismatic authority** refers to the unique talents and popular appeal possessed by an individual that make him or her particularly attractive as a public leader. These attributes may or may not be related specifically to the political arena (witness the election of Jesse "the Body" Ventura, a wrestler, to the Minnesota governorship in 1998); however, this is definitely an asset. **Legal authority** means that authority to govern is legitimated by the rule of law—that is, the laws and regulations

traditional authority
authority based on heredity, religion, or divine right

charismatic authority
authority based on the unique talents and popular appeal of an individual

legal authority
authority based on the rule of law

that must be obeyed by all members of a society, the rulers as well as those they rule. Thus a queen, president, prime minister, or former wrestler turned state governor is subject to the law. It is the law we trust and hence obey that legitimates the power of our leaders. Weber argued that modern bureaucracies are necessary parts of regimes whose power rests in legal authority.[3]

You can probably think of several examples in which one, some, or all of these sources of authority exist. Pierre Trudeau, for example, came to power in 1968 riding a wave of popularity known as "Trudeau-mania." Many observers pointed to a similar phenomenon when Quebec Premier Lucien Bouchard led the "Oui" forces in the last sovereignty referendum. Still, the reason that these leaders and others like them continue to govern after the hoopla has subsided is because this power is ultimately vested in legal authority.

Weberian theory contends that, by its very nature, legal authority relies on a bureaucratic organization in order to maintain itself. This is not meant to suggest that bureaucracies do not exist in other expressions of political authority; rather, Weber emphasized that legal authority cannot exist without a bureaucracy to support it. He went on to describe what he considered to be the fundamental components of an "ideal" bureaucracy, which could then be used to assess the development of systems of organization in the real world. While Weber himself cited eight separate components, more recent interpretations have consolidated these into four main areas:[4] hierarchy, continuity, impersonality, and expertise.

In this context, **hierarchy** refers to an organized system of labour where it is clear who reports to whom in a superior–subordinate relationship. **Continuity** means that the people working within the organization are full-time employees and can make a career out of what they do. **Impersonality** means that jobs and routines are based on written rules and records, which guard against favouritism. **Expertise** refers to hiring practices, which are based on merit rather than patronage, and the ability to control and access information and knowledge specific to a particular area. Weber concluded that the more closely an organization approximates these ideals, the more rational and efficient it will be. In short, organizational efficiency occurs when people are hired for what they know rather than for whom they know. And, as these employees work their way up through the ranks, they will develop expertise that can be used to improve the operation of the organization.

hierarchy
an organized system of labour characterized by a superior–subordinate relationship

continuity
the long-term or ongoing nature of a bureaucracy

impersonality
the objective nature of jobs and routines in a bureaucracy, based on written rules and records

expertise
knowledge of or ability in a particular area or subject

Criticism of Weberian Theory

The major flaw with the Weberian view of bureaucracy is that it attempts to explain this type of human organization by measuring it against an ideal, or perfect, model. Weber asserted that the closer a bureaucracy came to approximating this model, the more efficient it would become. This is often not the case in the real world. In fact, strict adherence to the Weberian model can sometimes result in a very inefficient organization. For example, hierarchy and continuity can deter initiative and produce apathy as workers begin to feel insignificant and underappreciated. Expertise and strict adherence to formal rules can create a work environment that detracts from the organization's overall aims as employees focus on career advancement rather than on collective organizational needs.

Formal rules that are put in place to ensure fair treatment for everyone may paradoxically achieve the opposite effect. For example, in the past many police forces required prospective officers to meet certain height and weight requirements. These criteria were seen as objective requirements of the job. However, these standards inadvertently discriminated against certain groups of people. Since the standards reflected the average for white males, women and some cultural minorities faced unintended discrimination if they chose a career in policing. An argument can be made that physical size is important in law enforcement; however, an equally compelling argument can be made for equality of opportunity for employment. Thus, rules that at first appear neutral and non-discriminatory may produce the opposite.

These criticisms aside, Weber's analysis does provide insight into organizational behaviour, and as we will discover later in this chapter, plenty of evidence exists to support his observations.

Structuralist Theory of Bureaucracy

Frederick Winslow Taylor (1856-1915)

Whereas Max Weber was interested in the general aspects of bureaucratic organization, Frederick Winslow Taylor focused on its key elements. Taylor wanted to find out how best to use human and mechanical resources—workers and machines—to maximize productivity and minimize waste. This approach is called **scientific management**.

scientific management
management approach based on using resources in ways that maximize productivity and minimize waste

A mechanical engineer by trade, Taylor began his career on the factory floors of late-19th-century America. These experiences prompted him to consider ways to improve the efficiency of factory work. His observations of the workers led him to draw two conclusions: (1) they were prone to slacking off, and (2) their jobs were inefficiently organized. Taylor argued that a scientific approach could be used to solve both of these problems, and the result would benefit both workers and employers. His method was to have a trained observer watch an above-average employee at his or her task, identify and time each component of that task, and then teach this method to others in similar jobs. This would provide an empirical, objective standard against which employers could measure employee productivity. Taylor proposed solving the awkward organization of the jobs themselves by rearranging them so that each worker would be responsible for one or two clearly defined tasks, rather than doing piecework, which was a common practice during his day.[5] As industrialism pervaded society, Taylor gained a considerable following, and in 1911, he published a book entitled *The Principles of Scientific Management*,[6] in which he outlined several theories of organization modelled on his ideas.

Criticism of Taylor's Scientific Management

Taylor's theories of scientific management have drawn criticism for several reasons. First, he asserted that there should be a clear distinction between management and labour. Implicit in this division was an assumption that managers should be responsible for setting standards and making decisions, which would then be carried out by workers. This has been referred to as the "strong back and weak mind" principle by some critics, who also point out that Taylor's approach prevents workers from having any meaningful say in the duties that are expected of them. To be fair, Taylor recognized the importance of cordial labour–management relations, but his ideas suggest that he believed proper results could be achieved only when management dominated the relationship.

Later theorists criticized this approach for its emphasis on strictly material rewards for workers who performed well. This one-dimensional, mechanistic view of workers as mere cogs in the factory machine was certainly not lost on workers themselves. Much of the labour unrest of the early 20th century occurred as a result of attempts to implement principles of scientific management without workers' consent. Thus, Taylor's view of labour as but one (expendable) resource in industrial capitalism cannot address the non-economic human aspects of work—such as job satisfaction, morale, and loyalty—as motivating factors that contribute to overall efficiency.

Human Relations Theory of Bureaucracy

Elton Mayo (1880–1949)

Problems arising from the top-down nature of hierarchical organizations (the approach embraced by Max Weber and Frederick Winslow Taylor) encouraged a search for other theoretical approaches in order to better understand individual organizational behaviour and find a way to maximize organizational efficiency. Through the work of a variety of individuals in business, psychology, and sociology, another perspective emerged known popularly as **human relations**. This approach recognizes the importance of attending to the personal and social needs of individuals to promote desired outcomes. Elton Mayo, a professor from Harvard University, was one of several researchers who applied this school of thought to the workplace. He is best known for conducting workplace experiments in 1924 at the Western Electric plant in Hawthorne, near Chicago. Along with two other researchers, Mayo hypothesized that improving workplace conditions (for example, lighting) would improve worker productivity. While the original experiments failed to achieve any conclusive results, they did lead to research into what became known popularly as the Hawthorne effect. Simply put, this principle states that workers who feel that they are appreciated and valued by their employers will be more productive.[7]

human relations
management approach that recognizes and addresses the personal and social needs of individuals

Mayo believed that modern industrial capitalism had disrupted more traditional forms of human support and interaction, such as family, community, and traditional work environments. These had functioned as informal meeting places for people and had facilitated feelings of identity and belonging. The modern workplace was not conducive to this informal social interaction, which was just as important a motivator as wages and career aspirations. In short, a workplace that is attentive to human needs results in better productivity. This can be achieved, Mayo argued, by involving workers in organizational decisions, teaching managers to be better listeners, and replacing overbearing supervision techniques with a more casual system of two-way communication.

Criticism of Mayo's Human Relations Approach

The human relations school of management drew criticism because its precepts appeared counterintuitive to the confrontational nature of labour–management relations. How much say should employees have in organizational decisions? What if these decisions run against those proposed by management? How much time and energy would have to be devoted to this exercise, and at what cost to organizational efficiency? For these and other reasons, the human relations approach has enjoyed limited success in the real world, although its influence is evident in such participative management strategies as management by objectives (MBO) and total quality management (TQM).[8] Still, there remains little evidence in the Canadian public sector that the human relations approach has been able to entrench itself in employer–employee relations. Many observers believe that during the heyday of organizational humanism from the 1960s to the 1980s, Canadian governments were still characterized by rigid hierarchies and job structures, little employee participation in decision making, top-down communication, and other elements of scientific management.

THEORY VERSUS PRACTICE: CONTRIBUTIONS TO PUBLIC LAW ENFORCEMENT

We have just completed a cursory survey of some of the fundamental theories that address the nature and function of bureaucracies, as well as how they can be managed to maximize efficiency and effectiveness. We can also employ these philosophies as analytical tools to study public law enforcement. As we will discover, each perspective contributes in different ways to an overall understanding of why and how the rule of law operates in Canada.

Marxist ideology is considered left-wing on the political spectrum. So, you might be tempted to conclude that in keeping with its tradition of active government social intervention Marxist thought should embrace large, well-funded police and military establishments. Recall, however, that Marxism—and the socialist sensibilities it spawned—harbours a deep mistrust of law enforcement agencies because they are the means by which those in power preserve their privileged positions. Although this reasoning may sound dated, its influence still permeates socialist views of society. Therefore, people on the political left favour a limited role for agents of state force. They prefer to focus public resources on remedying social inequities that they see as the root cause of crime and civil unrest. This way of looking at events is also used in other political contexts. For example, the pepper spraying of protesters at the Asia-Pacific Economic Cooperation (APEC) summit in Vancouver in 1997 could be viewed as use of force (RCMP officers) by the state (the Prime Minister's Office) to quash a legitimate expression of protest against perceived human rights violations by members of the public (student activists). Although Marxist analysis has faded somewhat from popular culture, it does offer a useful, if somewhat pessimistic, set of principles with which to judge the actions of politicians and bureaucrats.

Weber's ideas on bureaucracies give us a more rational view of the role of this type of human organization in society. Weber would recognize many of his bureaucratic ideals in today's complex system of public law enforcement. Officer ranking and the intricate reporting and communications networks among police forces demonstrate a clear hierarchy, providing opportunities for merit-based promotion in accordance with clearly articulated codes of professional conduct. On the other hand, in spite of possessing all of these traits, the system of law enforcement can fall prey to many of the criticisms associated with the Weberian model. For instance, who among the many chiefs of police in Canada would be willing to assert that the bureaucracy under his or her control is flawless? Again, the gap between theory and practice can at times be large, but there is little doubt that the intricate network of law enforcement in Canada represents a highly developed and modern society, just as Weber claimed.

Scientific management principles have become so much a part of private and public bureaucracies that most of us simply take them for granted. Managers search constantly for ways to improve the way tasks are accomplished given the resources available to them. For example, how should police officers be distributed across a city in order to maximize efficiency? To be fair to all citizens, officers might be assigned to patrol certain geographic areas, dividing the city into equal sections. But what if some areas have higher rates of crime? What about public education to prevent crime? As you can see, there are many variables at play in any given decision, and they all have implications for people inside and outside the organization. Still, scientific management continues to exert considerable influence. As a police chief, you may consult empirical data such as crime statistics to help you make decisions. You may draw on the experience of other jurisdictions to assess the success of techniques they have adopted to meet local challenges. In short, the essential elements of scientific management have become part of the management of all bureaucracies, including law enforcement.

As previously noted, the human relations school has not been adopted to any great extent in private or public administration. However, the importance of human resource departments and cooperative, team-based management strategies prove that this approach has not been totally rejected. Many government agencies whose members are exposed to dangerous or traumatizing events now provide crisis counselling and support to employees. Efforts like these suggest that this approach does in fact have benefits for an organization and its workers.

PRIVATE VERSUS PUBLIC ADMINISTRATION

"Why don't they run government more like they run business?" You have probably heard someone ask this question, or perhaps you have asked it yourself after hearing yet another media report of alleged government waste and inefficiency. Criticism of the public sector might lead you to conclude that the private sector's approach to bureaucratic organization is somehow superior to that of the public sector. As we will discover, however, this is a popular misconception that fails to recognize some unique characteristics of public administration and its mandate.

Government and private bureaucracies do many of the same things. Both manage large groups of people, overseeing a complex organization in an attempt to achieve certain goals. As well, both are engaged in budgeting and planning processes that facilitate these aims. Beyond these generalities, however, comparison becomes difficult. As public administration theorist William Sayre asserts, "Business and public administration are alike only in all unimportant respects."[9]

To begin with, the goals of private and public enterprises are different. In business, the ultimate aim is simply to maximize profit. This single pursuit informs every other decision an organization makes, from setting a price for goods and services to deciding what to pay employees. The ability of consumers to choose in the marketplace promotes competition among businesses that offer similar goods and services. By offering the lowest price or specialized products, a business hopes to attract an optimal number of customers. If it fails to make a profit, it goes out of business. Another way to explain this is to say that success in the private sector is based on **economic efficiency**, which refers to a business's ability to maximize profit and minimize expense.

economic efficiency
ability of a business to maximize profit and minimize expense

While economic efficiency may form part of the overall aim of public sector agencies, it is not necessarily a primary concern. This may at first seem wasteful, but a more detailed exploration may help you to see why economic efficiency may not be such a good idea in government. Government (and the bureaucracy that enables it to function) exists to respond to, maintain, and defend the **public good**. This term is more easily explained than defined, and refers to the complex fabric of publicly funded goods and services, available to all citizens, that provide for the operation of a modern civil society. National defence, education, and the justice system are just three examples of major social institutions that contribute to the collective

public good
the complex of publicly funded goods and services that contributes to the collective well-being of a state

well-being of a state. Most of us would agree that we need services such as these to continue to enjoy our nation's current standard of living.

There are several critical differences between public goods and services and those in the private sector. First, the aim in the public arena is to benefit everyone, regardless of their ability to pay for such goods and services. We all benefit from the roads, bridges, and hospitals in our communities. Many of these cannot be operated at a profit, and without public support they would simply not exist. Another good example is policing. There is general public agreement that all Canadians should benefit from the services of a police force, whether it is municipal, provincial, or national in its jurisdiction. Applying the rules of private enterprise in this case could well result in a patchwork system of law enforcement, because police forces would exist only in areas where their operations were economically profitable. This scenario, of course, is an unlikely prospect, but it does demonstrate that it is unfair to judge government services by economic values alone.

Other considerations that are absent in the private sector influence the provision of public services. It may not be efficient, for example, to provide all federal government services in both official languages, but in deference to equality and national unity this has been done. Regional issues and concerns can also influence policy decisions. Take, for example, the federal government's decision a number of years ago to decentralize and relocate many of its departments to various areas of the country. The economic costs of these moves were outweighed by concerns that all regions of Canada should benefit from the employment opportunities and economic benefits created by the presence of national ministries and departments.

Another major difference between the private and public sectors is in the area of accountability. Corporations are judged according to how much money they earn for their shareholders. As the chief executive officer, your failure to please this very select group of individuals could get you fired! Now, consider the number of people a cabinet minister has to please in order to be considered successful. Whether politicians or bureaucrats, individuals in the public sector find themselves accountable to the public in a way that their counterparts in the private sector never are. This scrutiny is magnified by opposition parties in the legislature and by the media, which continually question and criticize government policies. Our demands that governments properly account for how they spend our taxes results in a bureaucratic paper trail that can slow decision making and subsequent government action. You may want to keep this in mind the next time you have to fill out forms at a government office!

Efficiency Versus Accountability

There are other distinctions between public and private sector administration. For one thing, political and business timelines rarely coincide. Elections are held every four years or so, and that has an effect on what politicians try to achieve while in power and how they go about doing so. Business cycles and general planning horizons tend to be longer and less vulnerable to staff turnover. As well, public accountability and strict rules over hiring create a somewhat inflexible environment in which to manage personnel. This restrains public sector managers from behaving like their private sector counterparts, who are not subject to the same public accountability.

Why Privatize Public Institutions?

The debate over whether to privatize some government activity is not new. It stems from a larger political debate revolving around the nature and function of government in a society. From our earlier discussion of the political spectrum in chapter 5, recall that those on the left support public policies that favour social conscience and more government involvement as a solution to social problems, while those on the right argue for more individual responsibility and less government interference. The current debate surrounding privatization is simply another manifestation of this ideological conflict.

As right-wing policies have been adopted by the governing party at the national level, government has progressively cut the amount of money it gives to the provinces in the form of transfer payments. This, coupled with the election of right-wing governments in some provinces, has fostered an environment for all levels of government to consider privatization as an alternative to public service. The most common arguments for privatizing a public service are that it will save money and increase efficiency. Alberta Premier Ralph Klein's proposed privatization of health care and Ontario Premier Mike Harris's plan for private prisons are but two examples of moves to privatize parts of the public sector, and both politicians claim that the changes will save taxpayers' money while improving overall efficiency. But is this in fact the case? A growing body of evidence suggests that privatization may do neither. In the case of health care, critics point out that allowing private hospitals and clinics to compete alongside public ones can result in a two-tier system of health care—one for the rich who can afford better service, and one for everyone else. The danger, these critics argue, is that the private system siphons money and professionals out of the public system, because government still has to fund basic health costs and the best and brightest health care providers are lured to the private system by the promise of higher incomes. The result is that there is less money for public health care, which serves those people in society who are most at risk.[10] Further, because of the North American free trade agreement (NAFTA), once a sector of the economy has been opened to private interests, Canada cannot prevent foreign (especially American) companies from entering the field. Therefore, even if a province decides that privatization is a mistake, it may not be able to reclaim its role as the sole provider of public health care.

Prisons offer another good example of arguments for and against privatization. Supporters of private prisons contend that there are many examples to prove that private prisons can be cheaper to operate than government-run facilities.[11] Opponents, however, charge that private prisons derive much of their advantage from paying lower wages and cutting costs in areas that may endanger public safety. They cite instances where privatization ended up increasing the costs of incarceration rather than lowering them. In addition, public safety may be at greater risk because cost cutting can tempt private operators to hire fewer and less-qualified staff and to cut corners on equipment and facilities.[12] These concerns have led some communities to demand guarantees from governments that want to locate private prisons in their area, as occurred in Penetanguishene, Ontario in November 1999. When it first announced the construction of a "super-jail" there in 1997, the Ontario government promised that the facility would be publicly run. Its unexpected decision to invite private bids outraged many residents and led to threats from the town council that it might cut water and sewage service to the 1,200-person facility if the provincial government could not adequately explain the sudden change in policy.[13] (At time of publication, the council was still objecting but had learned that it was legally unable to prevent the provision of services.)

Supporters of private and public prison continue to argue the merits of their side, and it is difficult to know ultimately which side is right since every case is different. What we as the public have to consider, however, is whether society is any better off as a result of privatization. Should promised financial savings supersede the public good? Should we delegate this kind of state power to the private sector? Can a private company be held accountable in the same way as government? Is the move to privatize based on solid research, or is it simply a manifestation of right-wing political ideology? These are only a few of the many questions that need to be addressed in judging this recent shift in public policy.

SUMMARY

This chapter began by explaining what public administration is and briefly described its role in the overall scheme of government. Fundamental theories of bureaucratic organization help us to better understand why bureaucracies have become an essential part of all modern societies.

Karl Marx believed bureaucracies existed to legitimate inequities among social classes, while Max Weber saw them as central to the emergence of modern nation-states. Administrative pioneers such as Frederick Winslow Taylor and Elton Mayo changed the arrangement and management of tasks and people in order to maximize overall productivity. All of these theorists have had an impact on the nature and functions of bureaucracies and on those who are responsible for managing them. Each theory has contributed to a greater understanding of both private and public bureaucracies, although not all have enjoyed the same degree of acceptance in the real world. What is clear is that bureaucracies remain necessary, if often misunderstood, parts of civil society.

Comparing and contrasting the public and private sectors helps to illustrate what can happen when the rules of private enterprise are applied to public institutions. The results of such policy choices deserve further scrutiny to properly assess both the short- and long-term consequences for society as a whole.

KEY TERMS

bureaucracy	continuity
bureaucrat	impersonality
capitalism	expertise
traditional authority	scientific management
charismatic authority	human relations
legal authority	economic efficiency
hierarchy	public good

NOTES

1. The term "capitalism" refers to an economic system based on private ownership. Individuals or corporations use what they own (land, factories, etc.) to produce goods and services, competing with one another in the free market. This means simply that we as consumers are free to choose from among these offerings, based on such things as price, quality, reputation, and so on.

2. This set of principles is based on one found in David Kernaghan and David Siegel, *Public Administration in Canada*, 3rd ed. (Toronto: Nelson, 1995), 33.

3. Max Weber, *Economy and Society* (New York: Bedminster Press, 1968).

4. Gregory J. Inwood, *Understanding Canadian Public Administration: An Introduction to Theory and Practice* (Toronto: Prentice-Hall, 1999), 33–35. For earlier interpretations, see H.H. Gerth and C. Wright Mills, eds. and trans., *From Max Weber: Essays in Sociology* (New York: Alfred A. Knopf, 1970), 178.

5. "Piecework" refers to a method of employment where workers are paid for the amount they produce rather than for the amount of time they work. For example, the use of this practice in law enforcement might mean that as a police officer you would be paid according to the number of traffic tickets or people you arrested!

6. Frederick Winslow Taylor, *The Principles of Scientific Management* (New York: Harper & Brothers, 1911).

7. The experiments are explained in detail in F.J. Roethlisberger and William J. Dickson, *Management and the Worker* (Cambridge, MA: Harvard University Press, 1964).

8. In the management by objectives approach, employees set goals for themselves, in consultation with management, and their performance is measured against these goals. Total quality management is an approach that emphasizes a commitment to

quality throughout a company. Employees are seen as an important element in ensuring this quality in everything they make or do. The origins and consequences of these management approaches are explored further in Peter F. Drucker, *The Practice of Management* (New York: Harper & Row, 1954); George S. Odiorne, *Management by Objectives* (New York: Pitman, 1965); and W. Edwards Deming, *Quality, Productivity, and Competitive Position* (Cambridge, MA: Massachusetts Institute of Technology, Center for Advanced Engineering Studies, 1982).

9. Jay M. Shafritz and Albert C. Hyde, *Classics of Public Administration*, 3rd ed. (Pacific Grove, CA: Brooks/Cole, 1992), 3.

10. In Australia, which has a two-tier system of health care, the government has had to subsidize the private system almost $2.2 billion a year due to better than expected performance of public facilities and pressure from private physicians' groups. See Thomas Walkom, "Two-Tier Pain: Costly Lesson in Frustration," *The Toronto Star* (March 20, 2000), A1.

11. One group has estimated that cost savings could be as high as 23 percent. See Adrian T. Moore, "Corporate Corrections? Frequently Asked Questions About Private Prisons," available at http://www.rppi.org/prison/index.html.

12. A recent survey of private prisons in the United States has demonstrated that this may often be the case. See Kathleen Kenna, "You Better Be Damned Careful," *The Toronto Star* (November 28, 1999), F1.

13. See Roberta Avery, "Private 'Super-Jail' Meets Opposition," *The Toronto Star* (January 12, 2000), A4.

EXERCISES

■ MULTIPLE CHOICE

1. Public administration is concerned with

   a. deciding what the public wants

   b. making decisions for politicians

   c. managing government

   d. implementing the political will

   e. making decisions for citizens

2. Marxists see law enforcement officers as

   a. authorities whose work is legitimated by the rule of law

   b. agents of the privileged classes who exist to quash social unrest

   c. bureaucrats who are a necessary part of the machinery of government

   d. agents of the working class who exist to quash unrest among the privileged classes

   e. members of the bourgeoisie who hold a privileged position in society

3. According to Weberian theory, the three sources of authority in a society are

   a. legal authority, bureaucratic authority, and political authority

   b. traditional authority, scientific authority, and charismatic authority

   c. charismatic authority, hierarchical authority, and legal authority

   d. hereditary authority, legal authority, and traditional authority

   e. traditional authority, charismatic authority, and legal authority

4. The following result is inherent in attempting to achieve Weber's ideal bureaucracy:

   a. hierarchy encourages worker initiative

   b. hierarchy deters worker initiative

   c. hierarchy makes workers feel important

   d. hierarchy makes workers feel appreciated

   e. hierarchy makes workers focus on organizational needs

5. Under the scientific management approach,

   a. workers do piecework

   b. employers measure worker productivity against a subjective standard

   c. resources are used in ways that maximize productivity and minimize waste

   d. workers are responsible for only one or two clearly defined tasks

   e. c and d

■ TRUE OR FALSE?

_____ 1. Marx believed that government was necessary because it would eventually ensure that everyone would share equally in a country's resources.

_____ 2. A major flaw in Marxist thought is its inability to explain individual differences and the social mobility that takes place among members of different classes.

_____ 3. Traditional authority is authority that is legitimated by the rule of law.

_____ 4. In Weberian bureaucratic theory, "impersonality" refers to the nature of huge corporations that treat their employees like cogs in a machine rather than like people.

_____ 5. Success in the private sector is based on economic efficiency.

■ SHORT ANSWER

1. Define what is meant by "public administration," and describe its role in the political process in Canada.

2. What are the central elements of bureaucracy, according to the following theorists?

   a. Karl Marx

   b. Max Weber

   c. Frederick Taylor

   d. Elton Mayo

3. How might the above theorists view public law enforcement?

4. Using examples from current events, determine the effect these theories have had on both the public and private sectors.

5. Which of the theoretical approaches do you believe would be most effective in public law enforcement? Why?

6. Describe, in chart form, the differences between private and public administration.

7. Outline the proposed benefits of privatization. What are the potential drawbacks?

8. Do you agree with the Ontario government's decision to privatize some jails? Why or why not?

CHAPTER 7
Evolution of Public Administration

CHAPTER OBJECTIVES

After completing this chapter, you should be able to:

◆ Note the historical conditions that led to the development of public administration as a distinct field of academic study.

◆ Describe the evolution of the public service in Canadian history.

◆ Relate this evolution to broader social, economic, and cultural changes in Canadian history.

◆ Define and compare the advantages and disadvantages of the Keynesian approach to government policy.

◆ Define and compare the benefits and drawbacks of neoconservatism, noting its effect on Canadian public administration.

◆ Provide a general overview of today's public service in Canada.

> Guidelines for bureaucrats: (1) When in charge, ponder; (2) When in trouble, delegate; (3) When in doubt, mumble.
> —James H. Boren, American bureaucrat[1]

INTRODUCTION

The above satirical set of instructions for senior civil servants does little to challenge popular perceptions of the civil service. And yet, without these people our towns, cities, and indeed entire country would grind to a halt.[2] How did our public service wind up with such a tarnished reputation? One can argue that derogatory public attitudes toward politicians and bureaucrats have always existed. To a point, this is certainly the case. However, by examining the growth of the public sector in the context of larger historical events, it soon becomes apparent that recent criticism may have more to do with the larger currents of political culture than with actual ineptitude.

PUBLIC ADMINISTRATION AS MODERN ACADEMIC DISCIPLINE

Most scholars cite 1887 as a benchmark for the emergence of public administration as an academic discipline. It was in this year that future American president Woodrow Wilson wrote an essay entitled "The Study of Administration." In it, Wilson emphasized that a disciplined, academic study of public administration would result in more accountable and efficient government. Wilson wanted to make a clear distinction between the administrative and political elements of government because he believed that improving the former would correct corruption in the latter. This may seem a little odd given what you already know about the power of elected over non-elected officials in a democracy. Keep in mind, however, that Wilson wrote this paper at a time in American history when the political system of urban "party bosses" and vote buying was in its heyday.[3] As one of the first advocates of reform in this area, Wilson declared that only a professional bureaucracy—one based on formal rules of conduct and hiring practices based on meritocratic principles—could clean up existing corruption.

politics–administrative dichotomy

theoretical framework that views politics as the decision-making apparatus of government and administration as performing the implementation function

Wilson's ideas also laid the foundation for a theoretical framework known as the **politics–administrative dichotomy**. It views politics as the decision-making apparatus of government and administration as the implementation function of government. In other words, politicians should decide *what* to do, and bureaucrats should then figure out the most efficient means by which to do it. The main problem with this theory, of course, is that it is too simple. As we have learned, politicians and bureaucrats are inextricable parts of an overall process, and neither can claim exclusive ownership of public policy development. But while the concept in its pristine form has come under considerable criticism—it assumes, for example, that bureaucrats are politically neutral players in the art of government when in fact they are often central in the process of making public policy (see chapter 8)—it remains useful in some quarters, as we will see later.

While public administration quickly gained recognition as an academic discipline in the United States, Canadian universities were slower to grant it similar status in the realm of political science. In fact, no Canadian university offered a degree program in the field until just before World War II (at Dalhousie University in 1936). However, public administration became widely accepted in the years following the war to the point where today at least 16 Canadian universities offer degrees in public administration, some at the master's level.[4] Despite this success, in practice public administration has been subjected to severe public criticism in recent times. To see why this is so, we need to retrace its evolution in the context of Canadian history.

THE HISTORY OF THE PUBLIC SERVICE IN CANADA

As you learned earlier in this text, Canada's past reveals a lot about who we are and why our country's political system operates as it does. It is also important to keep in mind that outside events, issues, and trends have influenced the shape and direction of our political culture. The evolution of public administration in Canada can be used to illustrate both of these ideas.

Pre-Confederation

Before Confederation, colonial administration dictated the structure and operation of public service. Even 100 years after the decisive battle on the Plains of Abraham between the French and English forces in September 1759, the civil and political fabric of Quebec society retained the influences brought from France. Its bureaucracy reflected a hierarchically based military order, one steeped in patronage appointments doled out (or denied) by local authorities. The British colonies operated on similar principles, with delegates of the Crown rewarding those in the King's favour with government perks and positions. This practice remained commonplace after Confederation, but as Canada settled into nationhood, new challenges and ideas changed the nature and perception of the public service. One aspect of this came from Max Weber's "ideal bureaucracy" model (see chapter 6), which at that time was gaining popular acceptance in Europe and the United States.[5] Weber's ideal emphasized the importance of hiring people based on their qualifications rather than on who their friends were. Of course, the temptation to reward political allies did not disappear overnight, but as merit-based hiring became standard practice elsewhere, its advantages soon made themselves apparent to Canadian government officials.

The Minimalist State

As we will see below, Confederation heralded changes in the nature and size of Canada's public service. In comparison with today, however, the public service remained very small.[6] This can be partially attributed to beliefs at the time regarding the nature and function of government. Most people looked to their governments for defence and order and as a provider of infrastructure. All of these were ultimately in the interest of business, trade, and commerce, which were assumed to be the real power behind any great nation. While these pursuits did require some public administration, they were limited to what were considered essential or minimal services. This approach to government—common to Canada and most other nations at this time—was illustrative of a **minimalist state**—that is, state resources were used in the interest of the business, or capitalist, classes to promote individual wealth and economic growth. Social services such as health and welfare were deemed to be outside the

minimalist state
approach to government in which state resources are used in the interest of the business, or capitalist, classes to promote individual wealth and economic growth

realm of government, to be handled by private charities and individual philanthropists.

As the 19th century drew to a close and modern-day Canada began to take shape, the civil service began to grow, not only to keep up with the country's expanding geography but also to meet new demands brought on by the new challenges of urbanization and industrialism. While only 20 percent of Canada's population lived in urban communities of more than 20,000 people in 1867, this figure had increased to almost 50 percent by 1921.[7] Employment opportunities were created for such occupations as postal clerks, customs and excise officials, public educators, and public law enforcement personnel. These, as well as a host of other positions, presented alternatives to the traditional work of farming and other resource-based employment. The public service also offered the emerging middle classes opportunities to improve their economic position by moving up through the ranks of the public service, something they were unlikely or unable to achieve in other sectors. In short, the public service promised these people upward social mobility.

As we have already noted, this expansion in the public service was accompanied by a growing interest in the serious academic study of public administration. Likewise, Frederick Winslow Taylor's scientific management principles (discussed in chapter 6) were beginning to show up in the public sector in an attempt to find the "one best way" of managing its people and resources to achieve maximum efficiency. In response to challenges such as immigration and the settlement of the West, governments were increasingly forced to adopt Weberian principles of professionalism and hiring based on merit to ensure accountability and effective communication among the many departments, outposts, and employees being organized to carry out increasingly complex tasks. In 1908, the Canadian government created the Civil Service Commission, marking the drive toward a more professional civil service. It reinforced this trend by passing further reforms in this area in 1918. These laws went a long way in thwarting political interference in hiring practices by giving the commission the power to oversee all appointments to the public service. As well, candidates for jobs now had to compete for positions by writing exams and, once hired, were prohibited from any political activity. A new job classification system was introduced, and following World War I, special provision was made to favour returning soldiers for these positions. The 1920s witnessed little change in governments' approach to public administration, but events that would drastically alter the nature, philosophy, and function of both politicians and bureaucrats were on the horizon.

The Keynesian State

The years following the Great Depression and World War II marked a major change in the way government operated. Many events and people contributed to this shift, but it is commonly accepted that no one played a more significant role than British economist John Maynard Keynes. Keynes laid the theoretical groundwork for a conceptual transformation of the role of government from one of limited intervention to one of active intervention.

Keynes first came to prominence for his predictions about the harsh peace terms dictated to Germany after World War I.[8] The stock market crash of 1929 and the Great Depression that followed provided Keynes with another opportunity to pitch his unorthodox economic views. First, he asserted that traditional **laissez-faire**, or free-market, capitalism had led to the economic catastrophe of the 1930s; thus, the market could not and should not be left unregulated. Rejecting the tradition of minimalist government, Keynes also argued that government was the only entity capable of intervening in economic affairs, for only government had the power and public authority to do so.

Traditional economic remedies such as **protectionism** and **isolationism** seemed incapable of curing the economic misery for most of the 1930s, and although some Keynesian-style approaches were initiated, it wasn't until after World War II that they came into common usage.[9] At its heart, Keynesianism argued that government intervention in the economy was necessary to prevent the extreme economic cycles of boom and bust, with a view to reaching full employment. For example, when the economy was slowing down, governments could create temporary employment opportunities and spend money on public works to "prime the pump" of the country's economic engine to stimulate growth. Governments could also lower taxes and interest rates to encourage consumers and businesses to buy goods and make investments, thus further promoting a healthy economy and getting people back to work. Likewise, when the economy was drawing near to full employment and beginning to overheat, governments could alleviate inflationary pressure by raising taxes and/or interest rates. This cursory explanation greatly simplifies the Keynesian approach, but the widespread adoption of this philosophy in Canada and elsewhere after World War II had a dramatic effect on public policy and the civil service.

Accompanying these economic policy shifts was a growing public demand for government services in other areas of Canadian society. Taken together, these forces spurred growth in the public sector. Each new government program required staff, resources, and infrastructure, and as Canada's social safety net took shape during the 1950s and 1960s, the public sector likewise expanded to accommodate the increasing responsibility. Most of the initial recruitment took place through an affirmative action program that gave returning war veterans preference in hiring. Although this influx was to triple the size of the public service in Canada, it had little effect on public sector organization and operations. In fact, it wasn't until the baby boom generation entered the workforce in the late 1960s and early 1970s that a substantial transformation occurred. This new group of university-educated professionals saw themselves as more than just tools of policy implementation—they were also instruments of change, and as such should be actively involved in creating and evaluating public policy. These public servants were eager to apply current business strategies and the latest in technical analysis to the practice

laissez-faire capitalism
free-market capitalism (French for "leave alone")

protectionism
an economic remedy characterized by protecting domestic products with tariffs, import quotas, and other barriers to trade with other countries

isolationism
an economic remedy characterized by refusing to trade with other countries

of government, and as these skills became accepted, recognized, and respected, the public service in Canada greatly enhanced its power and influence within the political process.

Some critics feared that bureaucratic influences were threatening the integrity of the political process because unelected technocrats appeared to be supplanting the authority of elected representatives. Democratic principle dictated that politicians be held accountable to their constituents for the policy decisions they made, but how could this happen when these decisions were in reality being made by an unelected bureaucratic elite? This debate was only one among several that contributed to the emergence in the early 1970s of a political philosophy that drew on both new and traditional concepts of governance for its platform. As before, this development would result in dramatic changes in the nature and operation of the public service.

The Neoconservative State

stagflation
a situation where an economy experiences high unemployment and high inflation at the same time

The Keynesian welfare state came under increasing attack for both theoretical and practical reasons during the 1970s. First, a phenomenon known as **stagflation** cast doubt on the Keynesian economic strategy. Stagflation refers to an economic situation of high unemployment and high inflation at the same time, something that the Keynesian model had determined to be impossible. Second, the public began to lose faith in government's ability to solve social problems and increasingly viewed its activity as invasive, ineffective, and meddlesome. In addition, the media began to scrutinize the actions of government much more aggressively. Widely publicized political scandals such as Watergate in the 1970s (when US government officials, including then President Richard Nixon, used wiretapping and other undercover means to find damaging evidence against opposition Democrats) highlighted the potential abuse of political power and cast doubt on the integrity of politicians and bureaucrats. Stories of government waste and excess now received sensational media coverage, and governments faced mounting pressure to account for the tax dollars they spent. Collectively, the general public malaise with government that was characteristic of the mid-1970s led to calls for a return to a more traditional role for government. The ensuing ideological discussion eventually produced a hybrid political philosophy called **neoconservatism**. Neoconservatism ("neo" meaning new) criticized the Keynesian approach to government, arguing that government should revert to the limited role it had played at the beginning of the century, particularly in social and economic areas.

neoconservatism
a conservative political philosophy that argues that government should revert to the limited role it played at the beginning of the century, particularly in social and economic areas

new public management
an approach based on the belief that government has overextended itself by doing too much and becoming preoccupied with bureaucratic procedure

Neoconservative ideas prompted academics and others to search for new ways of thinking about government's role in society. What resulted became known as the **new public management** (NPM). The general premise of NPM was that government had overextended itself—that is, it was doing too much and had become preoccupied with bureaucratic procedure. As one source put it, government was doing "too much rowing, not enough steering"[10] in its pursuit of the public good. In practical terms, this meant shrinking the size and scope of government activity, deregulating various economic sectors, and privatizing the public sector in many jurisdictions. Neoconservative government first surfaced in Great Britain under Margaret Thatcher, then the United States during Ronald Reagan's presidency. In Canada, it was Prime Minister Brian Mulroney whose Progressive Conservative government introduced this new approach. The current federal Liberals under Prime Minister Jean Chrétien have continued this trend, and as we will see below, prolonged and even accelerated it.

The impact of neoconservative policies on the Canadian public service over the past two decades has been dramatic. Because of layoffs, budget cuts, and downsizing, the public service has not only shrunk in size but has also had to redefine itself to stay current and continue to meet the needs of all Canadians.

Today's Public Service

The public service in Canada has very little in common with its 1867 counterpart. Today its hiring practices are based on merit rather than patronage, and it is vastly more complex and professional. The goal, however, remains the same—to serve the public interest. So, who are the people behind the monolithic term "bureaucracy"? How are they organized? Let us begin by noting the difference between the public service of yesterday and today. In 1867, approximately 2,700 people worked for the federal government. Today, the federal government employs more than half a million Canadians in a variety of capacities. In spite of recent cutbacks, the municipal, provincial, and federal governments collectively employ almost one in four people out of a national workforce of nearly 15.6 million.[11]

Federal public servants work in one of six major occupational categories: operational, administrative support, technical, foreign service, administrative, scientific and professional, and executive. Each classification denotes certain jobs and pay rates, and these hold true for an employee regardless of the area in which he or she is employed. In addition to general qualifications, other factors such as language, regional interests, and equity affect the hiring process. These determinants reflect a desire on the part of government to respect the **theory of representativeness**. The theory asserts that a representative public service should include employees from all the major ethnic, religious, and socioeconomic groups in Canada. In other words, if the public service is to be responsive to the needs of all Canadians, it should represent a cross-section of Canadian society. For example, police forces across Canada want to attract more women and visible minorities to the profession to correct the overrepresentation of white males in their ranks. This aim has been criticized by those who argue that efficiency and effectiveness may be compromised by these initiatives. Should selection favour less-qualified candidates from underrepresented groups? Does one have to be from a certain background to be sensitive to the needs of people of the same background? The issue is complex, and the debate surrounding it will likely continue for some time.

theory of representativeness
theory that if the public service is to be responsive to the needs of all Canadians, it should represent a cross-section of Canadian society

Linguistic and regional representation have played a significant part in shaping who we are as a nation, and this in turn affects the public service. Federal government offices are distributed across Canada to equitably distribute employment opportunities and to provide a local presence for a central government that may be thousands of kilometres away. This manifestation of federal activity demonstrates to citizens that their taxes are, in fact, being used in their area. The historical importance of the French language and culture in Canada has already been noted, and it is for this reason that the federal government has actively recruited French Canadians to work in the public service. Up to the 1960s, English Canadians constituted the vast majority of federal public servants. Steps were taken to reflect the French presence in Canadian political culture. Through progressive policy action such as the Royal Commission on Bilingualism and Biculturalism of the late 1960s and the *Official Languages Act* of 1969,[12] the federal government succeeded in increasing the number of French Canadians in its public service. They now represent about 29 percent of the federal public service, roughly the same proportion of French-speaking Canadians in the general population.[13]

Federal public servants won the right to collectively bargain in 1967, long after this right had been granted to workers in the private sector.[14] The unionization of the public sector since then has resulted in some interesting dilemmas for the unions and the government. Unlike the private sector, where the interests of labour are pitted against profit maximization, collective bargaining in the public sector incorporates the dynamics of political power and the public good. We already know, for example, that governments raise revenues through taxation to fund public services. Therefore, it is the public that ultimately pays for any new expenses incurred as a result of negotiations taking place between government and a public sector union. Beyond this, however, lies a deeper implication. Some observers note that public sector unions may restrict or subvert government policy options by making demands that force their employer to do things it might otherwise reject. For example, a government may wish to give its citizens a tax cut or to cut its deficit and debt, but may be forced to abandon such an endeavour because of the increased wages and benefits it has just negotiated with a union. Further still, the precedent set by one union may serve as the benchmark for all other collective bargaining.

Although there is always a danger that this sort of policy manipulation may occur, for most of the 1990s public sector unions experienced far less success than did their counterparts in the private sector.[15] The recent restraint on salaries and the trend to downsize government have contributed to feelings of apathy and low morale in the public service,[16] and recent studies show that the public sector is experiencing difficulty in attracting people, who no longer see it as a challenging career option. This trend must be reversed if we are to preserve the integrity of public service in Canada.

SUMMARY

The evolution of public administration coincided with the development of a merit-based, professional public service in Canada. The nature and operation of the public service were also affected by socioeconomic changes taking place at home and abroad. Before World War II, Canada's public service existed within a minimalist state: government activity was limited in scope, so the public service was relatively small.

As the ideas of John Maynard Keynes took hold after the war, government's role expanded greatly as public demand for services increased and state involvement in social services became commonplace. The expansion continued until the early 1970s, when several events contributing to general public dissatisfaction with government resulted in the emergence of a hybrid political philosophy called neoconservatism. The practice of neoconservatism in the public sector, called the new public management, has led to a retrenchment of government activity in many areas and the privatization and deregulation of various sectors of the economy. The public service has thus undergone many changes since Confederation. It has evolved into a complex organization employing thousands of people that attempts to reflect a regional and cultural diversity that is uniquely Canadian.

KEY TERMS

politics–administrative dichotomy   stagflation

minimalist state   neoconservatism

laissez-faire capitalism   new public management

protectionism   theory of representativeness

isolationism

NOTES

1. *Oxford Dictionary of Quotations* (Oxford: Oxford University Press, 1992), 136–37.

2. A survey done in 1992 ranked public service at the municipal, provincial, and federal levels fifth, seventh, and eighth, respectively, in a study of impressions of service quality among eight private and public sector organizations. Insight Canada Research, *Perspectives Canada*, vol. 1, no. 4 (Fall 1992), 36.

3. This period in American history is referred to as the Progressive Era. It is perhaps most notable for the widespread reform of public services such as health, education, and welfare, particularly in urban areas. See Paul S. Boyer et al., *The Enduring Vision: A History of the American People* (Lexington, MA: D.C. Heath, 1990), 752–89.

4. Donald J. Savoie, "Studying Public Administration," *Canadian Public Administration*, 33, 3 (Fall 1990), 389–413.

5. Laurent Dobuzinskis, "Public Administration," in Michael Howlett and David Laycock, eds., *Puzzles of Power: An Introduction to Political Science*, 2nd ed. (Toronto: Oxford University Press, 1998), 156.

6. During the time of Sir John A. Macdonald, for example, the number of civil servants numbered only about 2,700. Ralph Heintzman, "Introduction: Canada and Public Administration," in Jacques Bourgault, Maurice Demers, and Cynthia Williams, eds., *Public Administration and Public Management: Experiences in Canada* (Sainte-Foy, QC: Les Publications du Québec, 1997), 4.

7. Alvin Finkel and Margaret Conrad with Veronica Strong-Boag, *History of the Canadian Peoples, Vol. 2: 1867 to the Present* (Toronto: Copp Clark, 1985), 12–19, 285.

8. Keynes was among the British delegation at the peace negotiations, and he argued against punitive measures against Germany. The ensuing hyperinflation that accompanied the drastic drop in value of the German currency and the rise of the Nazi party in Germany were seen as proof that he was indeed correct. See J.M. Keynes, *The Economic Consequences of the Peace* (New York: Harcourt, Brace and Howe, 1920).

9. One of the most widely publicized approaches was that carried out by US President Franklin Roosevelt, whose "New Deal" and its offspring "National Recovery Administration" attempted to influence wages, work hours, and prices. See Frank Friedel and Alan Brinkley, *America in the Twentieth Century*, 5th ed. (New York: McGraw-Hill, 1982), 221–61.

10. David Osborne and Ted Gaebler, *Reinventing Government* (Reading, MA: Addison-Wesley, 1992).

11. Heintzman, "Introduction," 5.

12. *Official Languages Act*, RSC 1985, c. 31 (4th Supp.).

13. Canada, Public Service Commission, *Annual Report 1999–2000* (Ottawa: Minister of Public Works and Government Services, 2000), table 2. Available at http://www.psc-ctp.gc.ca/annrept/ann9900_e.html.

14. Trade unions were illegal in Canada before 1872, and afterwards, governments remained reluctant to grant any meaningful right to bargain collectively. Leo Panitch and Donald Swartz, *The Assault on Trade Union Freedoms: From Wage Controls to Social Contract* (Toronto: Garamond Press, 1993), 17.

15. For example, a study comparing wage rates after inflation showed that Ontario public servants earned 6 percent less on their paycheques in 1997 than they did in 1992. In contrast, private sector

wage settlements averaged 2.6 percent raises in 1997. See Ontario Public Service Employees Union, "Payback Time for the Public Sector: Casselman," available at http://www.opseu.org/news/Press97/PressDec97.htm.

16. Stephen Thorne, "Public Servants Paying the Price for Job Cuts," *The Toronto Star* (April 22, 2000).

EXERCISES

■ MULTIPLE CHOICE

1. The politics–administrative dichotomy views

   a. politics as the implementation function of government

   b. politics as the decision-making apparatus of government

   c. administration as the decision-making apparatus of government

   d. administration as the implementation function of government

   e. b and d

2. The following factor(s) had an impact on the evolution of the Canadian public service:

   a. the urbanization and industrialization of Canada in the late 1800s

   b. events and issues in other countries, such as the United States

   c. growing public demand for government services

   d. theoretical ideas, such as those of Max Weber, Frederick Winslow Taylor, and John Maynard Keynes

   e. all of the above

3. Stagflation is a situation where an economy experiences

   a. high unemployment and low inflation at the same time

   b. low unemployment and high inflation at the same time

   c. low unemployment and low inflation at the same time

   d. high unemployment and high inflation at the same time

   e. no change in unemployment or inflation

4. Neoconservatism argues that

   a. government should intervene heavily in social and economic areas

   b. government should have a limited role in social and economic areas

   c. government should increase the size of the public service

   d. government should increase the scope of its activity

   e. government should regulate various economic sectors

5. The theory of representativeness basically holds that

   a. the public service should reflect the ethnic, religious, and socioeconomic diversity of Canadian society

   b. the public service can be more responsive to the needs of all Canadians if it represents a cross-section of Canadian society

   c. linguistic and regional representation in the public service is important

   d. a local presence for federal government, in the form of offices across Canada, is desirable

   e. all of the above

■ TRUE OR FALSE?

_____ 1. According to the politics–administrative dichotomy, bureaucrats should decide *what* to do, and politicians should figure out *how* to do it.

_____ 2. In the minimalist state, social services are not considered a responsibility of government.

_____ 3. The Keynesian model offers a solution to stagflation.

_____ 4. The new public management is a neoconservative approach to government.

_____ 5. Canada's official bilingualism is an example of the theory of representativeness in action.

■ SHORT ANSWER

1. What is the politics–administrative dichotomy? What is its major shortcoming?

2. Define "minimalist state." What factors led to changing this approach?

3. Explain the major concepts of the Keynesian welfare state. Why did this approach to government come under attack in the 1970s?

4. Explain the theory of representativeness in your own words, and give examples of how the theory is put into action.

5. How is politics involved in public service union collective
    bargaining? Why do public servants face more challenges in
    changing their work conditions than their private sector
    counterparts?

CHAPTER 8

The Art of Government: Making Public Policy

CHAPTER OBJECTIVES

After completing this chapter, you should be able to:

◆ Define the term "public policy."

◆ Describe the process of formulating, implementing, and evaluating public policy.

◆ Distinguish among a variety of policy instruments, and determine why governments choose to use one rather than another in a given situation.

◆ Using recent examples, analyze and assess the changing role of police associations in the public policy process.

[W]hat begins as a failure of perception among intellectual specialists finds its fulfilment in policy and action.

—Lionel Trilling, literary critic[1]

INTRODUCTION

How often have you heard politicians make promises at election time and then afterwards fail to achieve them? Jean Chrétien promised Canadians he would abolish the hated goods and services tax (GST) during the federal election of 1993, and yet close to a decade later it remains with us. It is easy (and to a certain degree, occasionally appropriate) to blame individual politicians for making promises they cannot keep. But it is too shortsighted and simplistic to conclude that the "say one thing, do another" phenomenon is a character flaw exclusive to politicians.

The foregoing raises some interesting questions about the process that shapes public policy. Why does it appear to most of us that there never seems to be any one definitive answer to problems facing government? This chapter will provide you with at least a partial answer to this question.

WHAT IS PUBLIC POLICY?

public policy
*what government does or
does not do*

The art of government is based on several key elements, among them leadership, integrity, and the ability to articulate an overall vision that has the support of the population. This requires a great deal of coordination, discussion, debate, planning, and evaluation on the part of officials. The result of this interaction produces **public policy**. Defining this term is a challenge, and there are several definitions to choose from.[2] Simply put, however, "Public policy is whatever governments choose to do or not to do."[3]

The relative ambiguity of this sentence is intentional. Public policy encompasses the "big picture"; it resists being distilled into a single act or law. In addition, public policy reflects what government does rather than what it says it will do. Statements made by politicians on a particular issue do not always produce policy. Again, however, public policy also reflects what a government chooses *not* to do.

MAKING PUBLIC POLICY

There are three fundamental stages to executing any exercise: formulation, implementation, and evaluation. The public policy process is no different. However, accomplishing these tasks within an organization as vast and complex as government constitutes a significant challenge for a number of reasons. Let's examine each step to see why this is so.

Formulation—What Is It We Want To Do?

The two major stakeholders in formulating, implementing, and evaluating public policy are politicians and bureaucrats. The relative power of each of these players can significantly affect the nature and shape of public policy. The theoretical continuum in figure 8.1 provides a general framework as to where policy originates and the effect this can have on government as a whole.

classical technocratic
a model of public policy in which decisions originate with politicians, who then provide bureaucrats with clear direction as to what should be done

At one extreme, known as the **classical technocratic** linkage, broad public policy decisions originate with politicians, who then provide bureaucrats with clear direction as to what should be done. This model draws on the Weberian bureaucratic ideal, where structure and communication are hierarchical and instruction is commonly understood and accepted. At the other extreme, the **bureaucratic entrepreneur** approach, bureaucratic experts within government come up with policy ideas, and then approach elected officials to obtain the resources and public legitimacy necessary to implement their programs. There are any number of points along this continuum sharing influence between these partners.[4] You may also have noticed that as one moves toward the bureaucratic side of the line, democratic input decreases.

bureaucratic entrepreneur
a model of public policy in which bureaucratic experts within government come up with policy ideas and then approach elected officials to obtain the resources and public legitimacy necessary to implement their programs

Although very simple, this model is useful because it helps illustrate that it is not politicians alone who are responsible for bringing policy ideas to public attention. Take, for example, recent moves toward a "law-

■ **Figure 8.1   Public Policy Continuum**

Classical
Technocrat

Bureaucratic
Entrepreneur

and-order" agenda by some governments in Canada, particularly that of Mike Harris in Ontario (see chapter 5). A classical technocrat analysis of this phenomenon might suggest that Ontario MPPs promised this as part of their election platform (which they did), or that public demand for this tough stand on crime has been brought to their attention. The politicians, in turn, put together a series of laws and programs and instruct the appropriate public servants (police, corrections, judiciary) to carry them out. If, however, the bureaucratic entrepreneur analysis is employed, the scenario changes. In this instance, one might imagine senior public servants in the above-mentioned areas seeking to gain approval for this policy shift. Thus, their aim would be to convince elected officials to promote the idea among the public that law and order is a desirable course of action. As you may have already guessed, several other actors also influence the policy-making process. The media may focus public attention on issues that in turn prompt some action or response by public officials. Interest groups and lobbyists may also intervene, providing input to advance or deter a course of action, or to propose alternatives.

Implementation—Let's Do It!

Once a policy decision is made, it must be carried out if it is to be of any use. Implementation refers to policy in action. It poses some of the biggest challenges for government, for it is at this stage that intent and consequence often become separated. As governments have been increasingly called to account for discrepancies between policies and subsequent actions and results by citizens, interest groups, and the media, they have begun to pay more attention to implementation. Leaving evaluation aside for a moment, let us consider some of the reasons implementation can fail to achieve desired aims.

With government as complex as it is, the margin for conscious and unconscious error in the areas of organization, coordination, communication, and time lag can alter the original intent or the ultimate success of a policy decision. Much has been written about these pitfalls and how to avoid them, but their detail is beyond the scope of this text. It may be easier to illustrate the message by using a scenario based on the earlier "law-and-order" example.

You have just been hired as a police constable in Goodville, a town of about 5,000 in a largely rural area of the province. Having been a diligent student, your knowledge of law and its enforcement extends beyond simple academics to include pertinent issues that affect your job. Reading the newspaper one morning, you observe that the premier has announced that the province is getting tough on crime. You think this sounds positive, but without specifics, you have no way to judge what this statement means to you and your profession. At the division, other officers and the chief discuss the policy but draw similar conclusions. Should your professional demeanour change? You decide that unless new directives are issued, you will carry on as usual.

A few days later, you are told that the province is drawing up legislation to articulate its policy, but the chief confides to staff that politicians are not listening to police chiefs and that she does not support the move. You hear from colleagues in other divisions that other chiefs are opposed as well. Meanwhile, the draft legislation has been criticized as being too costly by the finance department, so changes are being made that will save money but alter the bill's intent. The police chiefs are still unhappy and have recommended other changes to the bill. The media weigh in on the policy, pointing to falling crime rates and questioning the government's actions. After much tinkering and amendment, the bill is passed into law. Your chief declares that she will "interpret" the new legislation for the rank and file, but her perspective on some of its aspects seems to counteract its intent. To complicate matters, the staff and resources required to handle new tasks are being held up in legislative debate. By the time you receive a revised code of conduct, the government has decided not to pursue this matter because health care has become the focus of popular attention thanks to several media stories on the topic. Your chief is happy, but her abrupt retirement a few weeks later results in the appointment of someone who favours the government's abandoned initiative. It's all getting so political that you begin to wonder how anything is accomplished in government.

Before you throw up your hands in frustration, take some comfort in the fact that any large organization faces these challenges every day. But the task of getting things done in the private sector is less complicated than in the public sector. Public accountability and democratic sensibilities add layers of coordination and communication that necessarily encumber efficiency, and often by the time one policy choice has worked its way through the system it has changed or has an unintended consequence. Governments monitor this process through various stages and techniques of evaluation.

Evaluation—Did It Work?

Evaluation can be conducted during the implementation phase or following its completion—that is, once its outcomes are known. Evaluating the success of a government program isn't as simple as measuring tangibles, such as cost-effectiveness and efficiency, as might be done in the private sector. Because their ultimate goal is to serve the public good, government agencies must look for additional ways to evaluate what they do. Evaluation is all about accountability—demonstrating to interested parties that you are meeting organizational goals in a way that is acceptable to all concerned. In a private company shareholders tend to focus on profit, so evaluations, whether they are about customer satisfaction or corporate image, ultimately refer back to maintaining or increasing profit. As citizens, we demand accountability from governments because it is we who pay taxes that enable them to function. But measuring the effectiveness of public sector activity is not simply a matter of a financial cost–benefit analysis. As we learned in chapter 6, providing for the public good may mean operating some programs at a loss.

The other challenge facing public service managers is that it is sometimes difficult to identify specific criteria for measurement. How, for example, does one quantify national defence or measure the quality of justice? How would we know that these had improved over time? This problem of intangibility is not unsolvable, nor should it be used to justify abandoning any attempt at public accountability. However, it does highlight some of the challenges of public sector evaluation.

The success or failure of a policy initiative lies ultimately in the hands of bureaucrats. After all, they are the experts who have supplied much of the information necessary for their political masters to make these critical decisions. Likewise, the ability of public servants to present or withhold certain information in the formulation, implementation, and evaluation stages of the policy process places them at a distinct advantage over their political colleagues. As Reginald A. Whittaker notes:

> [I]t is the permanent officials who normally have greater access to information resources. Ministers, after all, are also MPs and party politicians who spend much of their time giving speeches, travelling, attending political functions, and engaging in activities quite remote from the business of their ministerial portfolios. In many cases, they have no previous training or experience in the policy fields of their departments, little time to gain such knowledge while there, and a relatively short span in one portfolio before they move on. … The bureaucracy, on the other hand, was there before, and will be there long after.[5]

The politics–administrative partnership Whittaker alludes to can be either creative or debilitating, yet it represents a key element without which government would cease to function. Evaluating government activity is one way of ensuring that both sides are acting in a responsible manner. As citizens have demanded more accountability from government, evaluation has become an important part of public sector programs. Public acceptance of policy decisions is one significant indicator of their success. There are several ways to monitor public compliance with government policy.

POLICY INSTRUMENTS AND DEGREES OF REGULATION

Once a policy decision is in place, governments have a range of options to choose from to ensure general compliance. Referred to as **policy instruments**, these are methods employed by governments to achieve their goals. The choice of instrument depends on a number of factors and can

policy instrument
methods employed by governments to ensure compliance with public policy and to achieve their goals

range from non-coercive inactive involvement (essentially, letting individuals and businesses regulate themselves) to coercive active involvement— in short, it is a question of the extent to which government wants to intrude into and influence private decisions.

This level of intrusion is best described on a continuum of state coercion (see figure 8.2). At one end, the state is largely absent from decision making. Individuals may be encouraged to voluntarily comply with a government objective. For example, municipalities might ask citizens to reduce the amount of water they use, for conservation reasons. Similarly, groups may be allowed to regulate themselves, such as in the case of the law and medical professions. Actions such as these cost very little and may signal relative indifference or reluctance on the part of the state to become involved in a particular area.

Next along the continuum are expenditure instruments, such as social spending (in the form of welfare, pensions, private sector assistance, and so on) or by offering tax breaks to encourage individuals and companies to change their behaviour. For example, a policy to reduce poverty among the elderly might increase social assistance payments to needy senior citizens. Likewise, people may be encouraged to save for their retirement through the creation of tax-sheltered retirement savings plans.

Regulation refers to the use of all civil and criminal laws of a state, including rules created by government agencies and dealing with taxation. It is at this point that public law enforcement begins to come into play. Governments may use police forces, the military, or both to coerce citizens to comply with certain policies, such as public peace and civic order. In more drastic circumstances, such as natural disasters or serious violence, governments may use public law enforcement agents to take control of private enterprises or restrict individual freedom. This final option is normally seen as a tool of last resort and is used for only a short time in democratic societies. One notable example occurred during the FLQ Crisis in Quebec in 1970.

Public ownership of certain enterprises is a method generally used when a product or service is considered essential for the public good. Thus utilities such as hydro, water, and telephone service are often publicly owned, although we are seeing a trend toward privatization. A police state is one in which democratic rights are taken away or do not exist. Such a state is usually run by a dictator or the army, or is imposed in a time of crisis. Canada witnessed such a measure during the FLQ Crisis, when hundreds of Quebeckers were arrested and detained without being told why and without any evidence that they supported the radical separatists.

Except during crises, it seems logical that policy makers usually choose the policy instrument that achieves the intended purpose for the least amount of resources, but they must also consider public perceptions. It may be cheaper to simply post speed limits on roads, but hiring police to enforce these limits is much more effective and is a choice of policy instrument that the public generally accepts. However, some experts contend that politicians make these decisions based on expected voter response.[6] Regardless, it should be clear that these choices have tangible

■ **Figure 8.2   Continuum of State Coercion**

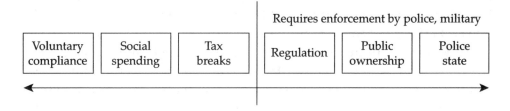

consequences for you, both as a citizen and as a professional in the field of law enforcement. This is because there is considerable flexibility within each policy instrument.

This flexibility allows governments to signal the importance of a particular policy in the overall context of their administration. They are restricted in this exercise by legal traditions, social norms, and current public attitudes on the subject. For example, lawmakers may implement a "get tough" policy on speeding by increasing fines for offending motorists. On the other hand, punishing these individuals by sentencing them to life imprisonment would be seen as excessive and could be characterized as cruel and unusual punishment. As conscientious police officers, how might you and your colleagues react if life imprisonment was the penalty? Would you be less vigilant in apprehending *all* speeders? This illustrates the necessity of common sense and prudence on the part of policy makers in order to secure willing compliance.

INFLUENCING POLICY FROM THE OUTSIDE: THE CASE OF THE TORONTO POLICE ASSOCIATION

Thus far, we have mostly limited our discussion of the policy process to two key groups—politicians and bureaucrats. In reality, of course, the process is vastly more complicated. Professional lobbyists, business and consumer groups, and a host of other stakeholders may enter and exit the process, depending on what issue is in the spotlight and whether a new initiative is imminent in that area.

Chapter 7 mentioned that unions can also affect public policy. Public sector unions represent workers who are employed, in effect, by taxpayers. Therefore, any improvements in the working conditions of these employees directly affect government revenue. If collective bargaining raises the cost of providing a public service, government may be forced to raise taxes or cut services in other areas to cover the increased costs. In addition, the right of most public servants to withhold service, or strike, as a pressure tactic may prevent the public from accessing some government services. There are limitations to this right—for example, police, fire, and ambulance services have been deemed essential to citizens, so these groups cannot go on strike. They can, however, resort to other means to achieve their demands, such as through work-to-rule campaigns or by appealing to public sentiment.

Recent developments in some Ontario police forces reveal a new and controversial tactic employed by some unions seeking to enhance their influence in politics and the policy process. Notable among these initiatives are those employed by the Toronto Police Association, the union representing Toronto's 7,000 police officers. The union, led by president Craig Bromell, has adopted an aggressive style to support its aims, an approach that Bromell himself has characterized as "bully" tactics.[7] The tactics include targeting politicians who disagree with the union on policing issues, hiring private investigators to dig up "dirt" on these individuals, and then using the information to silence or defeat them. Under Bromell, the union has also advised its members not to cooperate with the province's Special Investigations Unit (SIU), the civilian agency that investigates serious and fatal incidents involving police.[8]

Bromell has made no apology for using these aggressive tactics, saying that they are necessary to protect police from undue interference from civilian authorities who he claims have little idea of the reality of policing in Toronto. Other police associations have begun to adopt similar strategies, holding non-confidence votes on their chiefs and openly questioning budget and policy decisions in their municipalities. For example, in Ontario in the last two years Niagara Region, Durham Region, Guelph, Ottawa-Carleton, and Toronto have all openly questioned the leadership of their police chiefs.[9] This trend marks a significant departure from the traditional role of these groups. "Police associations ... are making it clear they are no longer content to just negotiate contracts and come to the aid of cops who get in trouble. Now, some of them want to dictate force policy—and determine who is chief."[10]

In late 1999 and early 2000, the Toronto Police Association initiated a fund-raising campaign to lobby for changes to legislation covering juveniles and repeat parole violators, and to subsidize the police association's endorsement of politicians who supported its law-and-order agenda. Depending on the amount contributed, donors were issued bronze-, silver-, or gold-coloured windshield stickers. The colours corresponded to donations of $25, $50, or $100, respectively. Questions arose over whether those with stickers would receive special treatment from police, particularly people who could afford the $100 gold ones.

Critics charged that the campaign was creating the impression that police service could in essence be bought, and that the union was intimidating and harassing those opposing its agenda. There were also questions about whether the union had breached regulations governing the political activity of police officers in Ontario. In late January 2000, the Toronto Police Services Board passed a bylaw banning True Blue following a unanimous condemnation by city council earlier the same day.[11] The union subsequently ceased the campaign, and pending lawsuits launched by the union and the Toronto Police Services Board have been dropped. However, the union says it will continue to engage in political activism.

Implications for Public Policy

These events present some interesting issues for us to consider. Most of us can empathize with the frustration expressed by police officers regarding the slow and seemingly ambiguous nature of the policy process. It can be unwieldy, and the consultation, coordination, and adjustment that occurs throughout the process can appear to defy logic and efficiency. To do otherwise, however, undermines the fundamental democratic principles of representative government and political accountability.

First, the very idea of democracy demands that a police force be subordinate to a civilian authority. Implicit in this doctrine is the understanding that attempts to subvert or intimidate that authority cannot be tolerated. Police forces that become accountable only to themselves risk abusing the power delegated to them by government by covering up misdeeds or by breaking the law themselves.[12]

Second, the civilian authority is made accountable to the people through legitimate elections. The perception that police may use their investigative power to blackmail or intimidate political "enemies" not only runs the risk of narrowing the field of candidates for political office, but may also result in less creativity and innovation in policy debate and direction. Finally, whether we favour or oppose particular government policies, few would argue that the means by which they were created lacks public credibility. As was pointed out in chapter 1, we abide by the laws of the land because we respect the legitimacy and authority of the state. If people are afraid that the police will get them for expressing different policy options or critical viewpoints, then it is no longer the public but the police who determine what is acceptable government policy, and we are left with a situation where the public no longer recognizes or acknowledges the supremacy of the rule of law.

Of course, we would like to think that this would never be tolerated in Canada. Nevertheless, the trend suggested by the recent actions of the Toronto Police Association demonstrate the need for students of public administration to seriously consider public policy implications posed by seemingly unrelated incidents such as the one just described.

SUMMARY

Public policy refers to the action (and inaction) of government in reference to a particular area of its operation. Public policy is characterized by an ongoing process of formulation, implementation, and evaluation that involves several actors both inside and outside formal government. Ultimately, however, it is the bureaucracy's job to implement the decisions resulting from these complex interactions.

Governments may choose from a variety of options when it comes to ensuring public compliance with particular policies. These can range from symbolic gestures, such as public information campaigns encouraging voluntary changes in behaviour, to rigid enforcement using police and the military. The policy instrument chosen depends on a number of factors, including the importance of the policy, current relevance, and necessity.

Public policy is a reflection of democracy in our society. The example of the Toronto Police Association's recent political activism illustrates the dilemma inherent in shaping and controlling public policy in a modern democracy such as Canada.

KEY TERMS

public policy

classical technocrat

bureaucratic entrepreneur

policy instrument

NOTES

1. *Oxford Dictionary of Quotations*, 4th ed. (Oxford: Oxford University Press, 1992), 702:18.

2. For example, see definitions by Peter Aucoin, "Public-Policy Theory and Analysis," in G. Bruce Doern and Peter Aucoin, eds., *Public Policy in Canada* (Toronto: Macmillan, 1979), 2; and Malcolm Taylor, *Health Insurance and Canadian Public Policy: The Seven Decisions That Created the Canadian Health Insurance System and Their Outcomes* (Kingston, ON: McGill-Queen's University Press, 1987).

3. Thomas R. Dye, *Understanding Public Policy*, 5th ed. (Englewood Cliffs, NJ: Prentice-Hall, 1992), 1.

4. Robert Nakamura and Frank Smallwood propose five major types of relationship in *The Politics of Policy Implementation* (New York: St. Martin's Press, 1980), ch. 7.

5. Reginald A. Whittaker, "Politicians and Bureaucrats in the Policy Process," in Michael S. Whittington and Glen Williams, eds., *Canadian Politics in the 1990s* (Toronto: Nelson, 1995), 429.

6. See for example Michael J. Trebilcock et al., *The Choice of Governing Instrument* (Ottawa: Economic Council of Canada, 1982), 27.

7. Bromell's statement to this effect in late 1999 on CBC televisions *The Fifth Estate* (February 2, 2000) was picked up by the media and subsequently became virtually synonymous with his leadership.

8. This has become common practice since Bromell assumed the presidency and has been characterized by many observers—including Bromell himself—as a direct challenge to civilian oversight of the police. Ibid.

9. Jennifer Quinn and John Duncanson, "Police Chiefs Feel Heat of Unions," *The Toronto Star* (January 14, 2000), A1.

10. Quinn and Duncanson, A1.

11. Paul Moloney and Bruce DeMara, "New By-Law Bans True Blue," *The Toronto Star* (January 29, 2000), A1.

12. There have been several instances—particularly in the United States—during 2000 alone where lapses in civilian oversight have resulted in police abuse of power. See Katherine Kenna, "L.A.'s Dirty War," *The Toronto Star* (March 26, 2000), B1. See also Stephen Handelman, "New Yorkers Have Good Reason To Fear Their Police Officers," *The Toronto Star* (February 29, 2000), A25.

EXERCISES

▪ MULTIPLE CHOICE

1. In the classical technocratic approach to shaping public policy

    a. policy decisions originate with politicians

    b. politicians give bureaucrats clear direction on what should be done

    c. structure and communication are hierarchical

    d. instructions are commonly understood and accepted

    e. all of the above

2. Evaluating public policy involves

    a. ensuring that politicians and bureaucrats are acting responsibly

    b. accountability

    c. measuring the effectiveness of public sector activity

    d. demonstrating that goals are being achieved in an acceptable way

    e. all of the above

3. One challenge of evaluating public policy is

    a. the numerous criteria that can be used for measurement

    b. the tangible aspect of results

    c. conducting a simple cost–benefit analysis

    d. focusing on profit

    e. the often unquantifiable nature of outcomes

4. An example of voluntary compliance is

   a. the Canadian Institute of Chartered Accountants setting guidelines for the behaviour of its members

   b. offering a tax break to anyone who puts money in an RRSP

   c. police enforcement of highway speed limits

   d. requiring a licence to operate a business

   e. requiring citizens to file a tax return

5. The following influence the policy-making process:

   a. politicians

   b. bureaucrats

   c. citizens

   d. the media

   e. all of the above

■ TRUE OR FALSE?

____ 1. The prime minister *not* abolishing the GST is an example of public policy.

____ 2. The relative power of politicians and bureaucrats can have a significant effect on public policy.

____ 3. At one extreme on the continuum of state coercion, individuals are encouraged to voluntarily comply with a government objective.

____ 4. Public law enforcement comes into play at the point on the continuum of state coercion where a society becomes a police state.

____ 5. As a basic democratic principle, a police force must be subordinate to a civilian authority.

■ SHORT ANSWER

1. What is public policy? Who are the key players in the process?

2. Briefly describe the process of public policy formulation, implementation, and evaluation.

3. What external factors can influence the nature of policy implementation? Give examples.

4. Relate the importance of policy evaluation to public accountability. How are the two connected?

5. What is a policy instrument? What factors influence a government's
    choice of instrument?

CHAPTER 9

The Bureaucratic Machinery: Government Operations

CHAPTER OBJECTIVES

After completing this chapter, you should be able to:

◆ Identify and explain the overall purpose of a government department and its role in the Canadian political system.

◆ Identify and compare a variety of other government bodies, including Crown corporations and regulatory agencies, and discuss their role in government operations.

◆ Analyze the nature and function of administrative law in relation to the activities of government.

◆ Discuss and debate concerns about government databases.

INTRODUCTION

Having surveyed the intricacies of the public policy process, the term "machinery of government" no doubt has greater meaning for you. Although this metaphor implies a somewhat negative image, it is useful if you imagine government as a series of organized components, each with a particular purpose, that are connected in some way to the greater whole. For instance, the Government of Canada is organized through the activity of departments, Crown corporations, and regulatory agencies, all of which make contributions to the public good. In this chapter, we will consider the nature and organization of each of these components to further demystify the process of public administration.

GOVERNMENT DEPARTMENTS AND WHAT THEY DO

When the Canadian government decides to undertake a new policy or launch a new program, it must decide what organizational form would best suit the task. One option is to create a **department** (or ministry at the provincial level). A government department is responsible for carrying out some aspect of government policy. For example, the Department of

department
government division responsible for carrying out some aspect of government policy

Health oversees public health; the Department of National Defence protects Canadians through the armed forces and fulfills many international responsibilities.

All departments are statutory bodies—that is, they exist because a law to that effect has been passed in Parliament. At the federal level, the prime minister decides the number and types of departments that are required. There are no formal restrictions, but past practices and current needs guide decision making in this area. In 2000, there were 23 federal departments, but the number has reached as high as 40.[1] As we learned in the first half of this text, the prime minister and the ministers—the heads of the departments—form the Cabinet, where political power is centred and key policy decisions are made.

Most federal Cabinet ministers are chosen from the pool of MPs elected to the House of Commons. This is in deference to the democratic tenet that states that senior representatives of the public interest must be held accountable to the people they serve—in other words, they must be elected. Each minister is responsible for the official activities of his or her department and is answerable to the public for both good and bad actions taken by the department. This fundamental principle of parliamentary government is called **ministerial responsibility**. It may be easier to think of this concept in terms of a hockey team. When the team is doing poorly, it is not the players who accept responsibility, nor are they the ones who are fired. As head of the organization it is the coach who assumes responsibility, and hence it is he or she who suffers the consequences. Likewise, even if the minister is personally unaware of departmental wrongdoing, it is the minister who resigns as a symbolic gesture to preserve the public's faith in the political process.

ministerial responsibility
principle of parliamentary government that makes ministers responsible for the official activities of their departments

Traditionally, the principle of ministerial responsibility has carried much weight in Canadian parliamentary affairs. However, recent events have led to speculation that it is losing credibility, both symbolically and in practice. This is because the size and complexity of many government ministries make it virtually impossible for one person to keep track of everything that is happening. Additionally, elections and prime ministerial discretion mean that Cabinet ministers are shuffled in and out of **portfolios** (another term for departments) fairly frequently, in contrast to the private sector.

portfolio
department

Consider, for example, the case of Human Resources and Development Minister Jane Stewart. Formerly the minister of Indian Affairs and Northern Development, she assumed the Human Resources and Development Canada (HRDC) portfolio in mid-1999 following a minor federal Cabinet shuffle. By November, stories had begun to surface about financial mismanagement of the Transitional Jobs Fund, an HRDC program that gives grants to promote job creation. Investigation revealed several serious problems, including political patronage, bureaucratic bumbling, and lax regulation. Much of the damning information arose from an internal audit going back to 1997, during which Stewart's predecessor, Pierre Pettigrew, was minister.[2] As the scandal grew in early 2000, opposition party calls for Stewart to resign became a daily occurrence despite her brief time in the position. At the time of publication of this book, Stewart remained the HRDC minister, while Pettigrew was international trade minister.

Strict adherence to the doctrine of ministerial responsibility dictated that Stewart resign, yet most of the activity in question predated her appointment. Similarly, when questions arose about possible mismanagement of the Ontario Realty Corporation (ORC), the provincial body responsible for managing property owned by the province, it was MPP Chris Hodgson, Chair of the Management Board of Cabinet, who was ultimately responsible for the agency's activities. The Management Board of Cabinet is the Cabinet committee that manages the Ontario government's staff, money, real estate, and other resources. Yet Hodgson refused to resign amid several allegations of ORC mismanagement and rumours of political patronage.[3] As you can see, there is some justification for re-examining ministerial responsibility. But to simply abandon it would effectively sever the relationship linking the actions of bureaucrats to the democratic accountability of their political masters and produce a dangerous lack of accountability on the part of the people we elect to represent us. The temptation to abdicate responsibility or shift blame in politics must be kept in check if public faith in the political process is to be preserved.

Deputy Minister

The deputy minister's position marks the point at which political power becomes bureaucratic action. Reporting to the minister (the political head of the department), the deputy minister (DM) is the most senior bureaucrat within that department. While the minister directs the department, the DM ensures that directions are carried out. As such, the DM acts as the go-between for the minister and the civil servants, conveying departmental policy and voicing employee concerns. As we saw in chapter 8, communication is ongoing between the political and administrative components of government; thus, the role of deputy minister is crucial in the realms of policy advice, dispute resolution, and human relations (the "people management" part of the job).

Although they report and are responsible to the minister of their department, deputy ministers are appointed by the prime minister. This may seem odd at first, but given the environment the justification for this is pretty straightforward. The relative transience of the Cabinet minister in any given portfolio puts departmental stability and continuity at risk (can you imagine having to switch course professors two or three times a semester?). Most DMs are career civil servants who have worked their way up through the ranks and have become experts in their particular area. Their consistent presence in the world of political change promotes efficient departmental operation and a reliable source of information and advice for ministers who are new to the job.

As the administrative heads of their respective departments, deputy ministers wield considerable power, some of it in law and some of it in tradition. For example, the *Interpretation Act*, a federal statute relevant to this topic, states that

24. (2) Words directing or empowering a minister of the Crown to do an act or thing, regardless of whether the act or thing is administrative, legislative or judicial, or otherwise applying to that minister as the holder of the office, include ...

(c) his or their deputy; ...[4]

In essence, this allows the minister to delegate a wide range of responsibilities to his or her deputy. DMs are also key players in the development of policy, advising the minister, recommending alternatives, and apprising the minister of expected public responses to and practical limitations of ministerial decisions.

Minister Versus Deputy Minister

While the minister–deputy minister relationship is characterized by mutual support, it is important to keep in mind the distinction. DMs cannot make regulations, answer to Parliament on behalf of the minister, or sign Cabinet memoranda. These restrictions aside, it is generally accepted that DMs will manage the day-to-day affairs of their departments, including supervising subordinates, tracking budgets, and performing other administrative activities. While ministers are free to intervene in departmental operations, these are usually left to the DMs. For one thing, Cabinet ministers are usually far too busy with other obligations to become overly involved with departmental affairs.[5] Thus, the degree to which ministers and their deputies venture into management and policy matters, respectively, varies according to their personality and preferences, and political necessity. This precarious balance can overwhelm deputy ministers, who often end up being overloaded with both managerial and policy responsibilities.

Before moving on, we should note a couple of important aspects characterizing the position of deputy minister. First, it is non-partisan. This means that DMs remain neutral in their duties, favouring neither a particular party nor its ideological beliefs. Rather, they serve the broader public interest of good government. Of course, this is easier to say than it is to do because of the politicized nature of policy development and the partisan agenda dictated by individual political parties in power.

Second, the post of deputy minister is insulated from direct public scrutiny by virtue of its relative anonymity. This is appropriate, given that it is the minister—an elected representative—who ultimately must accept responsibility for policy decisions in his or her department. Related to this is the knowledge on the part of DMs that in return for their frank and honest advice they will be shielded from public attention. Thus, one rarely hears of a particular deputy minister or other senior bureaucrat in relation to government policy matters.[6]

Classification of Departments

Given the diversity of government departments at the provincial and federal levels, it is sometimes difficult to grasp how they interact with

■ **Figure 10.1   Classifying Departments According to Service and User**

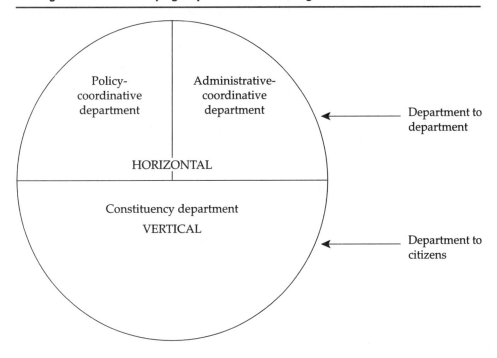

one another to coordinate and effectively carry out government policy. Political scientists use various categories to shed light on the inner workings and overall operation of the bureaucratic machinery.[7] Using these classification systems, we can develop a short series of questions to see where a department fits into the big picture (see figure 10.1).

Us or Them?

Who is the primary beneficiary of the service being provided? Departments exist either to help citizens directly or to assist other government departments. Those that provide services directly to citizens are called **constituency departments** and are considered "vertical" because they hand down services to citizens. These types of public services are the most visible and accessible to the public. For example, the federal Department of the Solicitor General oversees the national prison system as well as the operations of the Royal Canadian Mounted Police. Likewise, Human Resources Development Canada has offices across Canada that provide job search assistance, access to employment insurance benefits, and career guidance. Because they are universal in scope (available to all Canadians), these departments employ many people and have large budgets.

constituency department
department that provides services directly to citizens

Follow Them or Lead Them?

Departments that serve other departments are considered "horizontal" because they provide services within and through other departments. They can fall into one of two categories depending on whether they coordinate overall policy or facilitate it. Departments that coordinate policy

policy-coordinative department
department that coordinates policy across government

across government are called **policy-coordinative departments** or central agencies. They set the broad regulation and policy framework under which all other departments operate. For example, the Department of Justice may advise other departments on legal issues, while the Department of Finance can express federal priorities by shrinking or expanding a department's capital and operating budgets. **Administrative-coordinative departments** facilitate the operation of government services. They are involved in the less glamorous but necessary tasks of administration. For example, the Department of Public Works and Government Services looks after common departmental needs such as printing, office space, and purchasing.

administrative-coordinative department
department that facilitates the operation of government services

OTHER GOVERNMENT BODIES

Departments represent one means by which public policy is both developed, implemented, and enforced. Accordingly, circumstances may lead decision makers to choose other types of agencies, in order to achieve these ends. We will examine some of the alternatives common to the practice of public administration in Canada: regulatory agencies, Crown corporations, and boards and commissions.

Regulatory Agencies

Regulatory agencies defy a simple definition because they can vary so widely in size, authority, and scope. Traditionally, they were used to regulate the private sector (marketing, competition, pricing, and so on), but more recently they have also become involved in areas of social regulation (workplace safety, culture, environmental protection).

In spite of their differences, regulatory agencies share some common characteristics in how and why they carry out their function. They can be viewed as extensions of a ministry in the sense that each is ultimately answerable to a minister. Unlike ministries, however, regulatory agencies are insulated from direct political interference and therefore demonstrate to the public that official decisions are fair and based on objective criteria. Thus, these agencies are a means through which governments can influence a particular sector without undermining public confidence.

The legislation that creates regulatory agencies sets out the general rules by which they must operate. Some agencies are granted powers of **delegated legislation**, which means they have the ability to set and enforce regulations. In effect, political powers are handed down from the parent department, allowing an agency to make specific decisions that have the force of law.

delegated legislation
legislation handed down from a parent department that grants a regulatory agency political powers

Some agencies are empowered to grant licences or investigate incidents within their jurisdiction. For example, in Canada, communication-related industries are subject to rules enforced by the Canadian Radio-television and Telecommunications Commission (CRTC). The commission has the power to grant, review, and revoke broadcast licences as well as set fees for some telephone services. Given the influence of broadcast media on public opinion, it is easy to see why this power should not remain under the direct control of the governing political party.

As discussed in chapter 7, neoconservative ideology favours a limited role for government. This includes eliminating bureaucratic red tape in the form of government regulation of the private sector. A trend is under way, particularly under the neoconservative governments of Mike Harris in Ontario and Ralph Klein in Alberta, to do away with bureaucratic processes that may hinder private enterprise and limit economic growth. Commonly referred to as **deregulation**, the approach seems logical and has struck a chord with many people who view government regulation as overbearing and excessive. However, critics argue that in the rush to deregulate, short-term economic gains may be far outweighed by long-term costs. For example, there is evidence to show that Britain's deregulation of the cattle industry in the 1980s led to the outbreak of "mad cow" disease in the late 1990s because beef producers were no longer subject to strict health standards.[8] Closer to home, a five-year-long 40 percent budget reduction at the Ontario Ministry of the Environment, coupled with deregulation and downloading of water quality inspection, were cited as factors contributing to the outbreak of E. coli bacteria in the town of Walkerton's water supply.[9] While incidents such as these are relatively rare, they demonstrate what can happen when the long-term consequences of deregulation are negated or ignored. As citizens, we need to ensure that our politicians do not compromise public health and safety for the sake of short-term fiscal savings.

deregulation
reducing or eliminating bureaucratic processes that may hinder private enterprise and limit economic growth

Crown Corporations

Put tritely, Crown corporations are publicly owned businesses operating in the private sector and serving a public purpose. Like regulatory agencies, they are overseen by a ministry and are ultimately responsible to Parliament. Their distinctness arises from their corporate form and function. Crown corporations operate like any large private sector business, but because of their public accountability and legislated mandate, profit is often a secondary objective.

Why choose a Crown corporation to facilitate government policy? There are two basic rationales: economic and nationalistic. As we learned in chapter 2, Canada was born out of several diverse regional interests. Reconciling and accommodating these interests with overarching national goals has become part and parcel of the Canadian political process. Crown corporations provide the federal government with a vehicle to redistribute national resources and encourage public infrastructure. There are instances where provinces have used the Crown corporation models, albeit for similar purposes. For reasons of brevity and relevance, this discussion limits itself to the federal level. A Crown corporation can be created in an area of the economy where private business refuses to operate. By doing so, the new entity creates jobs and provides services or goods to an area that might otherwise go without. In addition, the corporation's presence in a community contributes to a sense of Canadian identity by connecting the area to a larger federal infrastructure.

A familiar illustration of the Crown corporation as "nation-builder" can be found in the Canadian Broadcasting Corporation (CBC). When created in the 1930s, its aim was to foster communication among and through the various regions of Canada through a network of radio—and later television—stations. The CBC's nationwide access requires staff throughout Canada, including regions such as the Far North, where private broadcasting would be unprofitable. The CBC is also an example of how the Canadian government has used the Crown corporation to limit or prevent the encroachment of foreign (read American) influence in an aspect of Canadian culture or economy.

The Crown corporation may also be chosen to put it at "arm's length" from possible political meddling, as noted in the previous section. By the same token, Crown corporations provide government with insight into the nature and current status of private sector actors engaged in similar activities. For example, Petro-Canada was created in the late 1970s to establish a public presence in the overwhelmingly foreign-owned energy sector.

One of the major drawbacks of choosing a Crown corporation as a policy vehicle is that, unlike private business, the corporation is ultimately answerable to political masters who in turn must account for that corporation's management decisions. For example, when CBC president Robert Rabinovich announced in the spring of 2000 his intention to eliminate local supper-hour newscasts, public outcry across Canada and the public admonition of several members of Parliament resulted in alterations to the original plan.[10]

The relatively recent trend toward limiting the role of government has prompted reconsideration of Crown corporations in their present form. Some right-wing critics have argued that they should be privatized (as were Air Canada and Petro-Canada) or eliminated entirely (as was the Cape Breton Development Corporation) because they compete unfairly in the private sector and are generally a waste of taxpayers' money. But this "slash-and-burn" approach not only ignores the historical context of the Canadian experience, but also assumes that private enterprise will assume the public interest for which the Crown corporation was originally intended.

ADMINISTRATIVE LAW

So far this chapter has been dedicated to outlining the structure and form of political and bureaucratic institutions and their role within the machinery of government. This section briefly surveys the legal parameters governing public institutions, with reference to protection and fair treatment of citizens.

Imagine for a moment that you are a police officer on highway patrol. You witness a car travelling at 50 km/h over the speed limit. You pull over the vehicle, walk up to the driver's side window, and ask for a driver's licence, registration, and insurance. The driver willingly complies, handing over all of the requested documents. Now consider the same scenario, except that this time your request for the three items is met with silence and suspicious gestures by the driver. Are your thoughts and responses different in this set of circumstances?

The second scenario can help to illustrate the concept of **discretionary power**—that is, the interpretive flexibility granted to a police officer as a government employee (in this case, an agent of public law enforcement) to act within a given setting. In the second scenario, you might decide that the driver is mentally unstable, doesn't like the police, or is having a bad day. This in turn influences how you will deal with this citizen. There is a procedure police officers must follow in roadside situations such as this one, but it would be virtually impossible for lawmakers to write down all of the potential variations. Thus, government delegates authority and responsibility to civil servants, who then interpret and abide by the set of rules handed down to them. This delegation is limited or controlled by principles of **administrative law**. This body of legislation (usually drafted by bureaucratic experts in a particular field) details such things as safety standards, applications for immigration, licensing requirements, and the process for appeals. These are the bureaucratic "rules of the game" to be followed by civil servants in their professional dealings with the public and with other government departments.

Although less visible than constitutional law, administrative law is bound by the same precepts and can be challenged in the court system. Laws can be ruled *ultra vires* (unconstitutional) if the Supreme Court finds that they in some way violate citizens' rights under the *Charter of Rights*.[11] For example, a directive from the provincial police instructing officers to stop all expensive sports cars and search drivers for drugs is a clear violation of the Charter rights of protection against unreasonable search and seizure and freedom from discrimination.

Principles of administrative law also preserve public faith in the rule of law by protecting citizens from unfair or arbitrary treatment by government agencies. In effect, administrative law acts as insurance that what is intended by politicians (as representatives of the people) ends up being implemented by bureaucrats in a just and equitable manner. The courts, through the process of judicial review, ensure this fairness. For example, a judge may rule that a regulatory agency has exceeded its authority by creating and enforcing rules that are outside its mandate or that go beyond the authority granted by its creators.

More directly, administrative law ensures that citizens affected by bureaucratic decisions have the right to due process and an appeal. This may include the right to represent themselves at relevant proceedings, the right to legal counsel and cross-examination, the right to be notified of hearing dates, and the disclosure of evidence held by the government body. In short, administrative law builds on the basic framework of constitutional law to ensure that governments and their delegates adhere to the rule of law in their day-to-day contact with the citizens they represent.

discretionary power
interpretive flexibility granted to some government employees to act within a given setting

administrative law
body of legislation that details the rules civil servants must follow in doing their jobs

When there is a dispute in this interaction, administrative law provides the protocol and forum necessary to resolve it.

SMILE, YOU'RE ON FILE

How much do you want your government to know about you? Although many Canadians have accepted government's collection of personal information as a part of life in the electronic age, new concerns were raised in 2000 when federal privacy commissioner Bruce Phillips revealed that Human Resources and Development Canada has a file containing as much as 2,000 bits of information on each of more than 33 million Canadian citizens. Among other things, the database contains information on education, marital status, employment history, income tax returns, records of social assistance, ethnic origin, and personal disabilities.

Critics fear that the privacy of citizens could be compromised, either through sale of the data to private companies or through misuse by authorities, because currently no laws govern how the information can be used. Statistics Canada is the only other government agency engaged in this type of data collection, but it is subject to strict laws and penalties to guard against abuse.

You might be tempted to dismiss this news as irrelevant to your situation as a student, but consider for a moment the possible implications. First, privacy is vital to a healthy democracy. Historically, it is one of the first rights to be violated by authoritarian regimes when they come to power. By removing privacy, they directly threaten citizens' abilities to think, act, and speak freely about government and other issues. This possibility was chillingly captured in George Orwell's novel *Nineteen Eighty-Four*,[12] where each and every detail of people's lives was monitored and scrutinized for conformity. In a way, history has proven Orwell correct. During the reign of the Nazis in Germany and Soviet communism in Eastern Europe, authorities routinely conducted surveillance of the private lives of citizens as a terror tactic. Of course, Canada is by no means similar to either of these repressive regimes, but the existence of such a detailed and expanding profile on every Canadian makes it possible to launch such action at some point in the future. Add to this database your record of Internet surfing and e-mail messages, and your dossier becomes that much more interesting and attractive to both friends and enemies.

Thankfully, the human resources minister has announced that the database will be broken up and guarantees will be put in place to ensure that every citizen's right to privacy is respected. In the meantime, smile—you're on file.[13]

SUMMARY

Government has been referred to as machinelike in its operation, and as citizens it sometimes feels like we are nothing more than numbers to the huge bureaucracy. The structure of bureaucracy in its various forms carries out government operations. The chapter began with an examination of government departments and ministers, highlighting the principle of ministerial responsibility, as well as surveying the power structure of a typical department. The deputy minister plays a critical role acting as the link between political and administrative power in the operations of government.

Departments are categorized according to who they serve and their purpose in the bureaucratic hierarchy. Constituency departments deal directly with citizens, while policy-coordinative and policy-administrative departments carry out functions among other government agencies. Regulatory agencies and Crown corporations serve different purposes, and they are two non-ministry bodies used by federal and provincial governments in certain circumstances to achieve policy goals.

Administrative law facilitates government activity. Part of its function is ensuring that government officials respect the rights of citizens and that disputes between the two groups are resolved in a just and equitable manner. Finally, government has a role in data collection, and this poses a possible threat for citizens' right to privacy.

KEY TERMS

department

ministerial responsibility

portfolio

constituency department

policy-coordinative department

administrative-coordinative
    department

delegated legislation

deregulation

discretionary power

administrative law

NOTES

1. This was during Brian Mulroney's first term in 1984. Organizational awkwardness necessitated the creation of an outer and inner Cabinet. For more information on the Mulroney approach to government, see Robert Bothwell, *Canada Since 1945: Power, Politics and Provincialism*, 2nd ed. (Toronto: University of Toronto Press, 1989), 433–44.

2. The audit, based on one-third of the total grant money handed out since 1997, found problems in 97 percent of the files examined. These included slipshod financial records and poor supervision of projects. See "Job Funds Fiasco Won't Fade Away Quickly," *The Toronto Star* (February 9, 2000), A24.

3. See "Land Scandal Tests Mike Harris' Ethics," *The Toronto Star* (May 10, 2000), A26.

4. *Interpretation Act*, RSC 1985, c. I-21, as amended.

5. Among the external duties of a typical Cabinet minister are collective Cabinet and party duties, constituency work, and attendance in the House of Commons, as well as representing Canadian interests abroad.

6. An exception to the principle of bureaucratic anonymity occurred recently when senior officials at Human Resources Development Canada responded publicly to Minister Jane Stewart's repeated attempts to blame "sloppy administration" for alleged mismanagement of department funds. See Graham Fraser, "Canada's Chief Bureaucrat Comes Out of the Shadows," *The Toronto Star* (February 26, 2000), K1; Allan Thompson, "Ottawa 'Sloppy' Over $1 Billion for Jobs," *The Toronto Star* (January 29, 2000), A1.

7. For specific approaches, see J.E. Hodgetts, *The Canadian Public Service: A Physiology of Government* (Toronto: University of Toronto Press, 1973), ch. 5; and G. Bruce Doern, "Horizontal and Vertical Portfolios in Government," in G. Bruce Doern and V. Seymour Wilson, eds., *Issues in Canadian Public Policy* (Toronto: Macmillan, 1974), 310–29.

8. The chain of events is explained in *Consequences: The Private Side of Britain* (Toronto: Indignant Eye Productions, 1998), a video documentary exploring the consequences of privatization under former British Prime Minister Margaret Thatcher.

9. The budget cuts resulted in one-third of ministry staff—many of whom were inspectors—being let go. The resulting lack of expertise and provincial testing have been cited as two of the potential causes of the tragedy. See Tanya Talaga et al., "Police Probe E. Coli Crisis," *The Toronto Star* (May 26, 2000), A1; and Royson James, "When the People You Know Don't Tell You About the Water," *The Toronto Star* (May 26, 2000), A8.

10. The plan represented an attempt by the CBC to deal with over $400 million in budget cuts ordered by the Chrétien government. Some observers argued that the changes were made to avoid embarrassing Liberal MPs in the year of an anticipated federal election. See James Travers, "Risking the CBC Body To Save a Limb," *The Toronto Star* (May 30, 2000), A25. For background, see Antonia Zerbisias, "CBC Local Newscasts Shrink—but Survive," *The Toronto Star* (May 30, 2000), A1.

11. *Canadian Charter of Rights and Freedoms*, part I of the *Constitution Act, 1982*, RSC 1985, app. II, no. 44.

12. George Orwell, *Nineteen Eighty-Four* (London: Martin Secker & Warburg, 1949).

13. For more detail on this issue, see Nahlan Ayed, "Ottawa Keeping Tabs on All Canadians," *The Toronto Star* (May 17, 2000), A3; and Valerie Lawton, "Ottawa Pulls Plug on Big Brother," *The Toronto Star* (May 30, 2000), A1.

EXERCISES

■ MULTIPLE CHOICE

1. The number of federal government departments is set by

   a. legislation

   b. the prime minister

   c. the House of Commons

   d. custom and tradition

   e. the Senate

2. The principle of ministerial responsibility means that

   a. a department is responsible for its official activities

   b. the prime minister is responsible for the official activities of a department

   c. MPs are responsible for the official activities of a department

   d. Parliament is responsible for the official activities of a department

   e. the minister of a department is responsible for the official activities of that department

3. The deputy minister is

   a. the most senior bureaucrat in the department

   b. the head of the department

   c. appointed by the prime minister

   d. a and b

   e. a and c

4. A constituency department

   a. serves other departments

   b. coordinates overall policy

   c. facilitates the operation of government services

   d. provides services directly to citizens

   e. all of the above

5. Crown corporations are

   a. privately owned businesses operating in the private sector and serving a private purpose

   b. privately owned businesses operating in the public sector and serving a private purpose

   c. publicly owned businesses operating in the public sector and serving a public purpose

   d. publicly owned businesses operating in the private sector and serving a public purpose

   e. publicly owned businesses operating in the private sector and serving a private purpose

■ TRUE OR FALSE?

____ 1. A deputy minister is a politician.

____ 2. Deputy ministers get their positions by belonging to the same political party as the government.

____ 3. Administrative-coordinative departments provide services directly to Canadians.

____ 4. Some government agencies have the authority to make specific decisions that have the force of law.

____ 5. A police officer who decides to search the car of a speeding motorist who is acting suspiciously is using discretionary power.

∎ **SHORT ANSWER**

1. Define and explain the purpose of a government department. What is its role in the Canadian political system?

2. Outline the roles and responsibilities of a minister and deputy minister. How do they interact with each other? Design an organizational chart showing the structure of a typical department.

3. What is a Crown corporation? How does it differ from a regulatory agency? Why do governments choose these forms rather than the departmental model?

4. What is administrative law? Explain its role in the bureaucratic process.

CHAPTER 10

Public Law Enforcement: Politics and Public Administration in Action

CHAPTER OBJECTIVES

After completing this chapter, you should be able to:

◆ Describe the functions of key government departments and their roles in the context of government and public law enforcement.

◆ Outline the general structure of a number of law enforcement agencies and how they are held publicly accountable.

◆ Discuss the case for judicial independence as a matter of public policy.

INTRODUCTION

Having established some of the fundamental principles of public administration and its relation to the political process in Canada, it is now time to see "where the rubber meets the road." In this chapter, we observe how government attempts to apply political and administrative ideals to the reality of public law enforcement. The situation is complicated by the inconsistent and arbitrary use of official names and titles to describe government bodies and the people who work in them.[1] Which departments do what, to whom, for whom, and with what consequences? As we will see, it is often a challenge to juggle cherished democratic principles with the cut and thrust of everyday law enforcement.

FEDERAL AGENCIES

Department of Justice

The Department of Justice has the primary responsibility for criminal justice policy at the federal level. It serves a dual purpose: to advise the federal government on legal matters, and to watch over the administration of justice in areas of federal jurisdiction. The department's responsibility to the federal government is referred to as the **attorney general function**, which means that it safeguards the legal interests of the federal government in any situation where the government has jurisdiction. As we know from our discussion of federal and provincial powers in chapter 2, this restricts the department's ability to act in some areas. Further, the Department of Justice provides legal advice to other federal government departments and agencies, and may represent their legal position in matters of regulation and litigation. The Department of Justice also prosecutes "violations of all federal legislation, other than the *Criminal Code*, in the provinces and for violations of all federal legislation, including the *Criminal Code*, in the territories."[2]

The second major responsibility of the Department of Justice is carried out through the **minister of justice function**. This relates to the more familiar duties of a ministry, such as creating, implementing, and evaluating, relevant policy, and overseeing the overall operation of the department. In the case of the Department of Justice, this refers to monitoring federal legislation, directives, and regulations to ensure that they do not violate citizens' Charter rights, and in general to considering "issues related to a fair and equitable justice system."[3]

As part of its mandate, the Department of Justice fulfills other responsibilities. It drafts and oversees the implementation of legislation in areas of criminal, family, and youth law, and it advises the federal government in such diverse policy areas as human rights, First Nations issues, and constitutional, administrative, and international law. These duties form part of the department's Administration of Justice Program, which is composed of three areas: government client services, law and policy, and administration.[4] The department's annual budget for 2000 was approximately $494 million.[5]

A justice minister performs a unique role in the federal Cabinet: he or she not only proffers political advice on legislative matters but also offers legal advice. The distinction is important because it is not unusual for one to be at odds with the other. For instance, a justice minister may express the opinion that gun control legislation is an unwise political move because it is difficult to enforce and is unpopular in certain areas, but at the same time the minister may advise the Cabinet that such legislation is well within the federal government's right to act.[6]

Many people are frustrated when they hear government officials say that they refuse to give their views on a hot political issue because it is before the courts. This is not simply a convenient excuse to avoid controversy, although it is often perceived that way. The refusal to comment is based on the legal principle known as **subjudicial rule**, which strictly prohibits government officials from commenting on an issue that is before the courts. The rationale is that, because they are closer to the process than normal citizens, officials' opinions might be perceived as tainting the judicial process, and thus may undermine public faith in that process. So the next time you are tempted to react cynically to "No comment," consider why the official has responded this way before judging his or her motives.

attorney general function
the function of the federal Department of Justice to safeguard the legal interests of the federal government

minister of justice function
the function of the federal Department of Justice to monitor federal legislation, directives, and regulations and to consider other justice-related issues

subjudicial rule
rule that prohibits government officials from commenting on an issue that is before the courts

Commissioner for Federal Judicial Affairs

In addition to the duties outlined above, the justice minister oversees the Office of the Commissioner for Federal Judicial Affairs. This body facilitates the operation of an independent judiciary—that is, it looks after judges' salaries, support, and training. The Office of the Commissioner acts as a guarantor of judicial independence by distancing judges and their work from direct political interference by the minister of justice. Its budget for 2000 was almost $262 million.[7]

Law Commission of Canada

The Law Commission of Canada (LCC) monitors the quality and relevance of Canadian law and legal institutions. Although the commission is ultimately responsible to Parliament through the justice minister, it can make recommendations to Parliament on such matters as law reform and renewal. The commission operates at arm's length from the government to ensure that any decisions it makes are not perceived to be tainted by the political party currently in power.

Most of the work done by the LCC is informative in nature—that is, it consults with the Canadian legal community, holds conferences, and conducts research into issues of law and justice. For example, it may survey lawyers or conduct forums on an area of law that no longer meets the needs of Canadians. In this way, the LCC acts as a legal-administrative watchdog, keeping Canada's system of law current, efficient, and effective. The LCC's budget for 2000 stood at just over $3 million annually.[8]

Department of the Solicitor General and Corrections

This department fulfills several functions in its mandate to manage the broad domains of justice and public safety in Canada. It employs more than 34,000 people and has a budget in excess of $2.5 billion.[9] Overall coordination is performed by the department, which supports the solicitor general and directs the work of four major agencies: the Correctional Service of Canada (CSC), the National Parole Board (NPB), the Canadian Security Intelligence Agency (CSIS), and the Royal Canadian Mounted Police (RCMP).

The department also includes a number of watchdog agencies that review and report on various aspects of public law enforcement and adherence to the rule of law. In this way, it seeks to demonstrate that the CSC, NPB, CSIS, and RCMP are accountable not only to political authority but also to public scrutiny.

Correctional Service of Canada

The CSC runs the federal prison system and is responsible for the custody and control of offenders sentenced to prison for two years or more. It has an annual budget of $1.3 billion. The CSC manages institutions across Canada that vary in security levels, and one of its prime goals is to rehabilitate offenders and prepare them for release back into Canadian society. It also supervises offenders who have been conditionally released—on day parole, full parole, or statutory release—to serve the last third of their sentence in the community.[10]

National Parole Board

The NPB exercises exclusive authority over the parole and conditional release of federal offenders (those imprisoned for two years or more). It also performs this function in provinces that do not have their own parole boards. (Quebec, Ontario, and British Columbia operate their own parole boards. All other provinces rely on the NPB to fulfill this function.)

The NPB decides whether to release (or, in some cases, pardon) individuals who have applied for parole, basing its decisions on such factors as prisoner records and risk assessment. In doing so, the NPB works closely with the CSC and the RCMP to share information and coordinate the supervision of successful applicants once they have re-entered Canadian society. The board has an annual budget of $25.5 million.

Canadian Security Intelligence Service

Created in 1984, CSIS monitors national security by collecting and analyzing information "on persons or groups whose activities may, on reasonable grounds, be suspected of constituting a threat to Canada's security."[11] The activities in question cover such things as espionage, sabotage, terrorism, and political subversion. The agency is also empowered to conduct security assessments of other government ministries, with the exception of the Department of National Defence and the RCMP, which do their own.

This mandate of CSIS is very broad and has caused some concern among civil rights advocates, who are afraid that its surveillance expertise may be used to investigate or intimidate political enemies of the federal government. In recognition of this concern, CSIS activities are subject to external review through a body known as the Security Intelligence Review Committee. This independent watchdog agency monitors CSIS actions and handles public complaints to ensure that the civil rights and liberties of Canadian citizens are being respected.

Royal Canadian Mounted Police

Since its creation in 1873, the RCMP (formerly the Northwest Mounted Police) has had a primary role in both federal and provincial law enforcement. Today the organization is involved in a wide range of activities, from battling organized crime to sharing expertise in and access to technology and information tools with other law enforcement agencies throughout Canada. As discussed in chapter 5, in addition to its national responsibilities, the RCMP performs provincial policing functions in all provinces except Ontario and Quebec. It works with First Nations to set up and encourage aboriginal police services on reserves, and it lends personnel and technical expertise for Canada's international peacekeeping responsibilities.[12]

The RCMP works with two external agencies to ensure public accountability and justice in its internal and external activities. First, public complaints about the conduct of members of the organization are handled by the RCMP Public Complaints Commission. The commission gives citizens an independent and impartial forum in which to present their concerns regarding RCMP officials' conduct.[13] Second, the RCMP External Review Committee provides members of the force itself with an independent forum for review in appeals of formal discipline, appeals of discharge or demotion, and other grievances forwarded to it.[14]

DEPARTMENT OF NATIONAL DEFENCE

As the department responsible for civilian oversight of Canada's military, the Department of National Defence (DND) serves two major functions. First, it directs the activities of the Canadian Forces (including the army, navy, and air force), which protect Canada from outside military threats and provide assistance in times of natural disasters and other domestic crises. Second, the department works closely with the Department of External Affairs to fulfill Canada's international obligations in the areas of peacekeeping and disaster relief abroad, and as a member of NATO. The department's annual budget is around $10.3 billion.[15] The defence minister has ultimate authority over the armed forces even though it is not he or she who actually plans or executes military manoeuvres. Maintaining civilian over military authority represents another hallmark of democratic government, demonstrating to citizens that the coercive power of the state is accountable. As noted in chapter 8, countries in which military power is no longer subject to civilian control are known as police states. Political regimes that use police or military power to violate democratic and human rights are also police states.

The Canadian Forces are managed by the chief of the defence staff, who works alongside a deputy minister. In this way, overall goals of the department are coordinated with those of the Canadian Forces. As with all departments, we find below these key players a complex bureaucracy of individuals who coordinate and carry out the many aspects of DND policy, whether these involve marshalling equipment for duty in Bosnia or coordinating sandbagging efforts during the Red River flood in Manitoba. DND's budget has been cut by 23 percent over the past decade, but recent budget increases have reversed this downsizing trend.[16]

PROVINCIAL AGENCIES

Due to the variety of structural approaches among provinces and territories, it would be too time-consuming to describe each one in detail. There are many similarities among them, however, so in the interest of brevity the following sections describe the ministries, agencies, and boards that make up the law enforcement system in Ontario.

Ministry of the Attorney General (Provincial)

In many respects, the attorney general can also be thought of as the provincial minister of justice.[17] He or she provides expert legal advice to the government and has overall responsibility for the administration of justice in the province. The statutory responsibilities of the attorney general are outlined in section 5 of the *Ministry of the Attorney General Act*[18] and can be classified into four broad areas: legal advice, civil litigation on behalf of the government, administration of the federal *Criminal Code*,[19] and administration of judicial affairs in the province.[20]

Like the federal Department of Justice, provincial attorneys general advise their respective governments in a number of legal and legislative areas. They scrutinize proposed legislation from other government ministries to ensure that it is legal, constitutional, and in conformance with accepted principles of justice.[21] The ministry also represents the province in cases of civil litigation where government interests or public rights are at stake.

An attorney general also has the power to legislate in the area of administration of the *Criminal Code*. This means that provincial governments carry out the process of criminal justice, while the federal government retains the ultimate authority to determine the actual content of the Code. Another interesting part of this process is that it is not the attorney general who decides whether to prosecute criminal offences. These decisions are left to the many Crown attorneys, who in turn do not begin this consideration until charges have been laid by police. Once again, basic principles of justice underlie this process. "The attorney general's responsibility for individual criminal prosecutions must be undertaken—and seen to be undertaken—on strictly objective and legal criteria, free of any political considerations."[22]

Finally, the Ministry of the Attorney General is responsible for the administration of a province's courts and its judicial affairs. The latter function is managed at arm's length by the Ontario Judicial Council, which operates in a manner similar to that of the Commissioner for Federal Judicial Affairs, described earlier.

As with the Department of Justice, note the difference between policy advice and legal advice given by a minister in this portfolio. The first is a matter of opinion, while the second is a matter of law. The principle of subjudicial rule also applies in cases of criminal and civil law.

Special Investigations Unit (Ontario)

Since 1990, municipal, regional, and provincial police forces in Ontario have been subject to an independent watchdog agency known as the

Special Investigations Unit (SIU). Created under provisions of part VII of the *Police Services Act*,[23] the SIU reports to the attorney general and looks into "circumstances involving serious injury, sexual assault, or death that may have resulted from criminal offences by police officers."[24]

Before the SIU's creation, police forces investigated themselves, or another police force conducted the process. This led to public concerns about integrity and objectivity, which eventually led to the creation of the SIU. The SIU has had limited success in carrying out its mandate, and there have been several calls from various law enforcement officials for reforms in this area.[25]

Ministry of the Solicitor General (Provincial)

This ministry oversees law enforcement and public safety in Ontario. Its activities are coordinated through the Office of the Solicitor General, which oversees the work of the Ontario Provincial Police (OPP), municipal and First Nations police forces, and several other agencies that provide police support and civilian supervision of police activity. Until June 1999, the Office of the Solicitor General also oversaw the operation of the Ontario prison system. Since then, corrections has become a ministry of its own, signalling a shift in government policy in this area.[26] The provincial solicitor general is also responsible for provincial and municipal police services and various aspects of public safety.

The Policing Services Division oversees the development of professional standards and training for policing in Ontario, and acts as government adviser and liaison to the police community. The ministry addresses public safety through regulation and fire safety services, the coroner's system, and emergency services. Recently in Ontario, there has also been a focus on victims' rights. The Victim Services Unit is responsible for policy development and victim assistance services in such areas as sexual and domestic assault.[27]

Ministry of Correctional Services (Ontario)

The Ministry of Correctional Services manages the custody of adult offenders serving sentences of less than two years or who have been granted parole by the Ontario Board of Parole. It also handles individuals awaiting transfer to a federal correctional facility to serve sentences exceeding two years, as well as 16- and 17-year-old young offenders. As with its federal counterpart, provincial corrections also manages a series of programs designed to help rehabilitate offenders and prepare them for reintegration into society.

Until recently, the ministry operated 42 adult and 5 youth facilities, but under current restructuring, the number of adult institutions will shrink to 22, being replaced by "super-jails" in Penetanguishene, Lindsay, and Milton. The ministry also supervises 127 probation and parole offices throughout the province and 50 open-custody residences for youths. The ministry has also opened a strict discipline facility for young offenders, popularly referred to as a "boot camp," and will open two more in the near future in Ottawa and southwestern Ontario. Approximately 73,000 adults and young people are under the ministry's jurisdiction on any given day. It currently employs almost 7,600 staff and has an annual budget of more than $500 million.[28]

Other Civilian Agencies and Police Services Boards

The Ministry of the Solicitor General also oversees several civilian agencies that monitor police activity in the province. One of these is the Ontario Civilian Commission on Police Services (OCCPS), an independent, civilian, quasi-judicial agency reporting to the solicitor general on the adequacy and effectiveness of policing services throughout Ontario. The OCCPS constitutes the highest level of civilian authority for chiefs of police, members of police services, and police services boards.[29]

The OCCPS handles public complaints about police policies, services, or officer conduct. It also conducts investigations into the administration of police services, hears police officer appeals from disciplinary decisions, and adjudicates budget disputes between police services boards and municipal councils.[30]

Communities with a local police force usually oversee its operation through a police services board. This civilian committee of municipal council works with the police chief to make policies, recommend budgets, and set priorities for the police force. The board also serves as an access point for public comments and complaints about police officers and their duties.

WHY ALL THE FUSS OVER JUDICIAL INDEPENDENCE?

A large part of the latter half of this text has been devoted to explaining the necessity of and democratic rationale for the supremacy of political authority over the bureaucratic process. Political authority is the means through which public servants are held accountable to the citizenry they serve. On the other hand, as we have noted in this chapter, some aspects of the justice system may supersede this principle in favour of fairness, objectivity, and freedom from political interference.

The principle was brought into sharp focus in the spring of 2000 in Ontario when a private member's bill was introduced by a backbench MPP. The proposed legislation, entitled the *Judicial Accountability Act* (Bill 66), would set up an annual registry of judges' decisions in criminal cases where maximum sentences exceed five years. Judges who give less than the maximum sentence for such crimes would have to explain their rationale.

The bill's sponsor, Scarborough Centre MPP Marilyn Mushinski, claimed that her bill would "motivate lenient judges to give out tougher sentences."[31] Mushinski is a member of the provincial Progressive Conservative Party led by Mike Harris, which as part of its neoconservative agenda has championed a "law-and-order" platform. Therefore, some observers were not surprised to hear the province's Attorney General Jim Flaherty voicing public support for the bill as it passed first and second reading in the legislature. However, the bill attracted severe criticism from a number of sources, including the legal community and civil rights organizations. They argue that it violates the fundamental democratic principle of judicial independence, which demands that the judiciary and the decisions of its members be free of political interference. They also argue that the bill creates a situation in which judges are forced to choose between principles of law and the partisan wishes of politicians currently in power.

We have already noted some of the ways in which the province's justice system is protected from perceptions of political manipulation (for example, the Ontario Judicial Council). We have also noted the crucial role of a provincial attorney general in this process. Thus, Flaherty's public endorsement of the bill raises serious concerns. After all, it is the sworn duty of this minister to ensure that all provincial legislation is constitutional and conforms to well-established legal principles. As a lawyer, Flaherty is bound by oath to protect the integrity of the courts. As attorney general, he alone in Cabinet is sworn to defend the constitution. Legal experts charge that Mushinski's bill is neither.

At time of publication, the bill was before the Justice Committee of the Ontario Legislative Assembly, and indications were that it would be left to lapse on the order paper, which means that it would die at the conclusion of the session of the Legislature. Still, that the bill got this far illustrates the need for constant vigilance to ensure that justice is preserved. As one source points out, it is imperative that political authority not alter bureaucratic action: "To make judges accountable to political opinion is to turn justice into mob rule."[32]

SUMMARY

This chapter has given you an opportunity to apply your knowledge of the structure and process of politics and public administration in relation to public law enforcement. Examining the respective powers of federal institutions such as the Department of Justice, the Ministry of the Solicitor General and Corrections, and the Department of National Defence demonstrates how each contributes to the overall system of justice and law enforcement at the federal level. The various watchdog agencies illustrate how these federal government institutions attempt to ensure fairness, accountability, and sensitivity to public concerns.

The federal bodies have their counterparts in provincial institutions such as the Ministry of the Attorney General, the Ministry of the Solicitor General, the Ministry of Correctional Services, and the many agencies and boards that have been put in place to monitor the activities of key actors within the government in general and the justice system in particular.

The balance between judicial independence and political accountability is sometimes difficult to achieve, but we must never lose sight of the fundamental principles that make up the justice system and ensure our rights as citizens.

KEY TERMS

attorney general function

minister of justice function

subjudicial rule

NOTES

1. For example, the words "ministry" and "department" may have the same meaning, while "commission" is used to describe agencies of varying size, function, and importance, making categorization by name alone virtually meaningless. Organizing agencies according to function is a better alternative.

2. Mary Ferguson, ed., *Federal Guidebook: A Guide to the Canadian Federal Government and Its Decision-Makers, 1999–2000* (Perth, ON: J.K. Carruthers, 1999), 43:1–43:2.

3. Ibid., 43:2.

4. Ibid.

5. Canada, Department of Justice, *Department of Justice 1999–2000 Estimates* (Ottawa: Department of Justice, 2000).

6. Despite a constitutional challenge from a majority of the provinces, the Supreme Court ruled in favour of the federal government on this subject on June 15, 2000.

7. Ferguson, 25:1.

8. Ibid., 44:1–44:4.

9. Solicitor General Canada, "Overview of the Department of the Solicitor General Canada," available at http://www.sgc.gc.ca/eoverview.htm.

10. For spending estimates and personnel, see Ferguson, 29:1–29:9.

11. Ibid., 20:1.

12. For more detail, see ibid., 70:1–70:6; and RCMP, http://www.rcmp-grc.gc.ca.

13. Details on current initiatives and other material available in Ferguson, 72:1–72:3.

14. Ibid., 71:1–71:3.

15. Ibid., *Federal Guidebook*, 50:1.

16. In his 2000 budget, Finance Minister Paul Martin promised $1.7 billion in new funding for DND over the next three years. See D-Net Online, "Budget 2000," http://www.dnd.ca/menu/budget/index_e.htm.

17. In fact, the federal minister of justice also holds the title of federal attorney general, although this term is rarely used.

18. *Ministry of the Attorney General Act*, RSO 1990, c. M.17.

19. *Criminal Code*, RSC 1985, c. C-46, as amended.

20. A detailed analysis of these responsibilities is available at Ministry of the Attorney General, "Roles and Responsibilities of the Attorney General," http://www.attorneygeneral.jus.gov.on.ca/html/AG/agrole.htm.

21. Because of the sensitive nature of this decision-making process, these considerations are delegated to the Office of Legislative Counsel to avoid allegations of political interference.

22. Ministry of the Attorney General, "Roles and Responsibilities of the Attorney General."

23. *Ontario Police Services Act*, RSO 1990, c. P.15, as amended.

24. Special Investigations Unit, "Our Mandate," available at http://www.siu.on.ca.

25. For example, in 2000, *The Toronto Star* reported that a document from the Ontario Association of Chiefs of Police outlined that body's wish to "strip the SIU of some of its powers, including recommending to the attorney-general that investigations be conducted by police officers seconded to the civilian agency." Bob Mitchell, "SIU Gets a New Home Amid Fight Over Powers," *The Toronto Star* (June 17, 2000), B4.

26. As noted earlier, the head of government (in this case, the premier of Ontario) has the power to create or eliminate ministries as he or she sees fit.

27. Ministry of the Solicitor General, "Policing Services," "Public Safety," and "Victim Services," available at http://www.Sgcs.gov.on.ca.

28. Information from documents obtained from the Ministry of Correctional Services, Communication Branch, June 2000.

29. Brockville Police, "Public Complaints," available at http://www.recorder.ca/police/PublicComplaints.html.

30. Ibid.

31. Quoted in Theresa Boyle, "Tory Bill Denounced as 'Judge-Bashing,'" *The Toronto Star* (May 6, 2000), A7.

32. "Scary Bill," *The Toronto Star* (May 6, 2000), H6. For more information, see Ian Urqhart, "Judges Bill a Strikeout for the Tories," *The Toronto Star* (May 17, 2000), A33; and Theresa Boyle, "Lawyers Slam Bill as Attack on Judiciary," *The Toronto Star* (May 16, 2000), A7.

EXERCISES

■ MULTIPLE CHOICE

1. The Department of Justice

   a. monitors the quality and relevance of Canadian law and legal institutions

   b. watches over the administration of justice in areas of federal jurisdiction

   c. advises the federal government on legal matters

   d. a and b

   e. b and c

2. At the federal level, the minister of justice function involves

   a. considering issues of fairness in the justice system

   b. monitoring federal legislation

   c. commenting on issues that are before the courts

   d. a and b

   e. b and c

3. The rationale for the subjudicial rule is that

   a. some cases before the courts are hot political issues

   b. politicians need a convenient way to avoid controversy

   c. public faith in the justice system is undermined by politicians' comments

   d. officials' opinions might be perceived as tainting the judicial process

   e. all of the above

4. Civilian agencies monitor police activity

    a. to give objectivity to investigations of alleged police misconduct

    b. to ensure the integrity of policing

    c. to report to the solicitor general on the adequacy of police services

    d. to report to the solicitor general on the effectiveness of police services

    e. all of the above

5. Judicial independence ensures a judiciary that

    a. is free from political interference

    b. makes decisions based on the principles of law

    c. is not influenced by the wishes of politicians who are in power

    d. is fair and objective

    e. all of the above

■ TRUE OR FALSE?

____ 1. The federal Department of Justice performs both the attorney general and the minister of justice functions.

____ 2. It is not unusual for justice ministers to find that their political advice contradicts their legal advice.

____ 3. The attorney general is responsible for deciding whether to prosecute criminal offences.

____ 4. Government attempts to influence the professional actions of judges contravene the principle of judicial independence.

____ 5. The existence of the Office of the Commissioner for Federal Judicial Affairs is one way of guaranteeing judicial independence.

■ SHORT ANSWER

1. Outline the broad mandate of the Department of Justice. How does it protect the federal justice system from political interference?

2. Compare and contrast the roles of the solicitor general and the justice minister at the federal level. Who is considered the chief law officer, and why?

3. What criterion determines whether an offender is sent to a federal correctional facility? What factors do you think should be considered when assessing an offender's application for parole?

4. What are the key differences between solicitors general at the federal and the provincial levels?

5. Make a case for or against the creation of a separate federal department of corrections. Do you agree with Ontario's rationale for having instituted this change? Why or why not?

6. What is the justification for civilians overseeing the police? Do you agree with it? Explain.

7. Under what circumstances do you think governments are justified in actively influencing the justice system? What risks do they take in this regard?

8. Outline some of the ways in which governments attempt to protect the independence of the judiciary. Why is this so important?

PART IV

Bringing It Home

CHAPTER 11

Don't Just Sit There— Do Something!

CHAPTER OBJECTIVES

After completing this chapter, you should be able to:

◆ Understand how an understanding of politics and public administration can enhance your personal and professional life.

◆ List some activities in which you can participate as a citizen in order to better understand and appreciate the political process.

◆ Assemble an intellectual "toolbox" to help you analyze and understand a variety of political issues.

> No one pretends that democracy is perfect or all-wise. Indeed, it has been said that democracy is the worst form of Government except all those other forms that have been tried from time to time.
>
> —Winston Churchill[1]

INTRODUCTION

With all of the negative news stories we are exposed to on a daily basis, it is tempting to dismiss politicians and the political process as irretrievably corrupt and hopelessly inefficient. One reason for this may be that so many of our political opinions are based on sensational media reports that tend to simplify complex political issues and emphasize particular types of stories, such as personal scandal and fiscal mismanagement. While the media no doubt play a critical role in keeping governments accountable to their constituents, it can be argued that the power they have to manipulate the political process presents an equal danger.[2] If we as citizens are to hold our elected representatives accountable for their actions, we need to familiarize ourselves with the process, procedures, and constraints under which they operate.

As a constituent, you may believe that your role in the political process is simply to vote when there's an election. In a democratic country such as Canada, voting is indeed one of the fundamental privileges of being a Canadian citizen. However, leaving it at that misses the point of this book, which is to acquaint you with politics and help you to make informed decisions about the people, parties, and processes that characterize the Canadian political system. Hopefully, having come this far, you feel more attuned to the world of politics. However, like many people, you may also feel powerless to do anything about what is going on in the world of government and politics. This chapter suggests some ways you can begin to make a difference while honing your political acumen in the process.

COMMON EXCUSES FOR AVOIDING POLITICS

When first confronted with politics, many students admit that they are confused, intimidated, or disgusted by the subject, or a combination of the three. This is not surprising given popular stereotypes and mass media's obsession with scandal. Hopefully, with the knowledge you have gained from this book and the course it represents, you will be able to critically analyze political events in a way that informs both your personal and professional life. Below are a few of the most common excuses given for avoiding politics, and some counterarguments.

Politicians Are Corrupt

This is a throw-away generalization that not only irks most politicians but is also unfair and untrue. The vast majority of politicians are honest, hardworking individuals who dedicate themselves to public life in order to benefit their constituents. It is to their credit that they continue to serve in spite of the negative stereotypes reinforced by the popular media. Politics reverses the popular adage "No news is good news," for we rarely learn from the media that politicians are doing a good job. This rebuttal is not intended to be an indictment of all media, for they too serve a purpose as watchdogs over public affairs. But the industry's tendency to simplify and shorten news stories may mask the complexity of some issues and thus misstate the issues. In any case, it's important not to approach the subject of politics from a cynical perspective. Keep an open mind and realize that, ultimately, politics is the art of compromise.

It Doesn't Affect Me

Nothing could be further from the truth. When it comes to politics, ignorance is *not* bliss. Law enforcement students sometimes believe that political issues not directly related to policing are of no concern to them. The reality is that it is virtually impossible to isolate the impact of political decisions. Government spending in one area may mean cutbacks in other areas or an increase in taxes to cover the extra cost. For example, spending more on health care may mean cutbacks to environmental programs such as water quality. The end result may be that contaminated water sources end up increasing health costs more than the amount of the cutbacks. These connections extend through municipal, provincial, and federal levels of government. Having a sound knowledge of the relationship among these many political actors allows you as a citizen to form opinions in a context that then informs the decision you ultimately make come election time. As well, this knowledge can help you understand the decisions made by others that affect your day-to-day work life.

They Break Election Promises

Economist John Kenneth Galbraith once described politics as the art of "choosing between the disastrous and the unpalatable."[3] Admittedly, politicians as a group are not known for keeping promises, but they should not be blamed exclusively for this shortcoming. As you have learned in the second half of this text, pledging to do something and then actually accomplishing it poses significant challenges in the world of public policy. In addition, the contemporary game of politics requires that issues be simplified so that they appeal to as many voters as possible. This approach can backfire, however, when it comes to actually implementing the promised solution to a problem.

DAZED AND CONFUSED?

Politics is by no means an easy science to grapple with. Changing events, players, and circumstances render useless any hard and fast rules and formulas. Understandably, this can intimidate some people. However, you can take some steps toward overcoming this feeling.

1. Keep up on political events. Warnings aside, tuning into ongoing media coverage of current events will help to familiarize you with the people, policies, and priorities of the day. Reading one or two newspapers a day is a great way to do this.

2. Discuss current political issues with friends. Talking over coffee or while walking home tests your understanding of events and exposes you to perspectives that are different from your own.

3. Make it a point to inform yourself at election time. Attend all-candidates' meetings, ask questions on subjects that concern you, and base your vote on the information and impressions you have gathered. Yes, some effort is involved, but it will have been well worth it when you finally cast your ballot as an informed citizen.

GETTING INVOLVED

Folk singer and social activist Pete Seeger once observed that bringing people together for any purpose is an act of politics.[4] Seeger made the comment in reference to people in his community who were organizing to clean up the Hudson River. By volunteering, you accomplish several purposes. First, you gain valuable experience that contributes to your résumé and hence future job prospects. Second, you learn how to work in cooperation with others to achieve a common goal. Finally, you open yourself to different viewpoints and career options through the contacts and experience you acquire. As a result, you will broaden your political horizons and develop a much better sense of your community and the many others who are a part of it.

Volunteer opportunities abound, and you should decide first what interests you and then pursue opportunities in that area. If you are not sure where to start, contact a community volunteer placement centre or consult the *Yellow Pages* under headings such as "Volunteer" and "Social Service Organizations." Many coaching positions are also available in local youth sports leagues. These are valuable references for anyone considering a career working with young offenders.

To be directly involved in politics you might consider becoming a candidate for municipal government, but many other avenues of participation are open to you if you are interested in formal politics. Survey the various political parties in your area to find out whether your political views tend to complement one particular party's platform (but be careful not to look for the "perfect" party—remember, politics is the art of compromise). You can join a party, help at the constituency office, or assist in party-sponsored events. Elections provide excellent opportunities to volunteer and make contacts in your community that may be of help to you later.

If you are concerned about a specific issue, you may wish to join a related interest group. There are many active groups in Canada supporting a huge variety of causes. Neighbourhood Watch, Road Watch, and Block Parents are just a few examples of organizations interested in civil peace and respect for the law. There are a host of socially oriented causes in the areas of environmentalism, poverty, and social justice. You can also attend local council meetings and forums that focus on particular issues of local concern. Again, elections provide many opportunities of this nature, including all-candidates' meetings and party rallies.

As you can see, the opportunities are out there for you to get involved at whatever level is comfortable for you. Make your choice according to the amount of time and energy you have available. Volunteering demands some commitment if you and the organization are to derive any benefit from it, but remember that the rewards to yourself and your community are directly related to the amount of time you invest.

AN INFORMED STUDENT'S INTELLECTUAL TOOLBOX

A recurring theme of this text has been to stress the importance of your responsibility as a citizen in the political process. Below are some tips to help you enhance your own intellectual toolbox. You'll also find a Quick Reference Checklist at the end of this chapter.

Tune In, Turn On ... Talk Out

Earlier, we cautioned you to be wary of the popular media because of the way they package news items. Still, there are ways to overcome this obstacle. First, when sizing up an issue, consider a variety of media (print, radio, television, Internet). Within each medium, individual providers reflect specific areas of the political spectrum in their news coverage and general viewpoints. For example, newspapers such as *The Globe and Mail, National Post,* and *The Toronto Sun* represent right-wing conservative positions, while *The Toronto Star* reflects a left-of-centre liberal approach to current events. Each also markets itself to a different target audience to attract a certain niche of advertisers. *The Toronto Sun,* for instance, is written at about a grade five reading level and is aimed more at moderately educated working-class readers, while *The Globe* and the *National Post* are written at a postsecondary reading level and are targeted at the well-educated wealthier upper class. These distinctions can be a little more subtle in other mainstream media, but by observing how and what each presents you should be able to figure out where they fit on the political spectrum and what audience they're trying to appeal to.

Assess a Source's Credibility

A good rule of thumb when listening to political messages is not to trust anyone who's over-wordy. Don't allow yourself to be snowballed by slick presentations or sources that play to your emotions alone. Mentally step back and examine the argument being presented and the evidence being given to support it. Is the source quoting specific, credible data or making sweeping general statements without backing them up? Thinking about research in this way will help you to base your own opinions on solid evidence rather than on emotion alone. You can add the latter to your viewpoint once you have made up your mind on an issue.

Keep an Open Mind

Try to keep an open mind when considering political issues. You may initially favour one side over another, but don't let these prejudgments turn to prejudices. Allow yourself some time to gather the facts and determine whether they counter your initial reaction. Open-mindedness in politics is not about having any opinion; rather, it is about listening to opposing viewpoints, weighing and challenging their credibility, and then drawing conclusions. Employing this strategy helps you to avoid being pigeonholed into one or another position before you have had a chance to explore the details of an issue.

SUMMARY

This chapter has presented some of the reasons people are frustrated by or avoid politics and has attempted to confirm the importance of constituents in the political process. Getting involved in politics means more than simply casting a vote in an election—it can mean doing volunteer work for a political party, becoming informed about political issues and party platforms by attending all-candidates' meetings, or simply keeping up on political events through the mass media. No matter what your level of involvement, a greater understanding of the political process and current issues can enhance your personal and professional life, and can help you to make a more informed decision when it comes time to cast your ballot.

NOTES

1. *Oxford Dictionary of Quotations*, 4th ed. (Oxford: Oxford University Press, 1992), 202:23.

2. One of the most prominent scholars to explore this phenomenon is Noam Chomsky. See Edward S. Herman and Noam Chomsky, *Manufacturing Consent: The Political Economy of the Mass Media* (New York: Pantheon Books, 1988); and Noam Chomsky, *Necessary Illusions: Thought Control in Democratic Societies* (Toronto: Anansi, 1991). The latter is available as an audio lecture from the 1989 CBC Massey Lecture Series (Toronto: CBC Enterprises, 1989), at http://masseylectures.cbc.ca/M_Chronology.htm. For related subject matter, see Chomsky's *Secrets, Lies and Democracy* (Tucson, AZ: Odonian Press, 1994).

3. John Kenneth Galbraith, quoted from a letter to American President John F. Kennedy, March 2, 1962. *Oxford Dictionary of Quotations*, 297:3.

4. Seeger made this comment on a live album recorded with Arlo Guthrie entitled *Precious Friend* (Warner Brothers, 1982). Preamble to "Sailin' Up, Sailin' Down," side one, track seven.

EXERCISES

■ MULTIPLE CHOICE

1. Media coverage of political issues can be coloured by

   a. a tendency to simplify and shorten news stories

   b. a focus on the negative while ignoring politicians who are doing a good job

   c. the commentator's position on the political spectrum

   d. the medium's attempt to appeal to a particular audience

   e. all of the above

2. Becoming better informed about politics and political issues can help you

    a. make better decisions as a voter

    b. understand how political decisions affect your personal life

    c. know more about your community

    d. understand how political decisions affect your professional life

    e. all of the above

3. Making an informed decision about any issue involves

    a. going along with whatever your friends say

    b. gathering information from credible sources

    c. sticking with your first reaction to the issue

    d. taking a cynical attitude toward anything you read or hear

    e. tuning out anything you don't agree with

■ TRUE OR FALSE?

_____ 1. Politics has no effect on your life.

_____ 2. Politics has no effect on public law enforcement.

_____ 3. Carrying out election promises is a significant challenge in the world of public policy.

_____ 4. One way to prevent being confused by politics is to keep up on political events by reading newspapers regularly.

_____ 5. Casting your vote at election time is one of your basic democratic rights.

■ **SHORT ANSWER**

1. Make a short list of some possible volunteer activities that interest you. What types of questions would you want answers to before considering each of these opportunities?

2. Would you consider running as a candidate for public office? Why or why not?

3. When considering political issues, why should you consult a variety of news sources?

4. How have your views of politics and public administration changed since you began reading this text? Give at least three specific examples.

5. Fill out the chart on the following pages as a reference for future inquiries.

QUICK REFERENCE CHECKLIST

Member of Parliament (MP)

Name: _____ Political Party: _____

    Phone: _____ Fax: _____ Web Site: _____

    Mailing Address: _____

    _____

    Constituency Office Location: _____

Member of Provincial Parliament (MPP)

Name: _____ Political Party: _____

    Phone: _____ Fax: _____ Web Site: _____

    Mailing Address: _____

    _____

    Constituency Office Location: _____

Municipal Government

Local Councillor

Name: _____ Ward: _____

    Phone: _____ Fax: _____ Web Site: _____

    Mailing Address: _____

    _____

    Constituency Office Location: _____

Mayor/Reeve

Name: _____ Political Party:_____

    Phone: _____ Fax: _____ Web Site: _____

    Mailing Address: _____

    _____

    Constituency Office Location: _____

Director of Education

Name: _____

    Phone: _____ Fax: _____ Web Site: _____

    Mailing Address: _____

    _____

    Constituency Office Location: _____

Local School Trustee

Name: _____ Ward: _____

    Phone: _____ Fax: _____ Web Site: _____

    Mailing Address: _____

    _____

    Constituency Office Location: _____

APPENDIX A

The Canadian Charter of Rights and Freedoms

PART 1 OF THE CONSTITUTION ACT, 1982

Whereas Canada is founded upon principles that recognize the supremacy of God and the rule of law:

Guarantee of Rights and Freedoms

1. The Canadian Charter of Rights and Freedoms guarantees the rights and freedoms set out in it subject only to such reasonable limits prescribed by law as can be demonstrably justified in a free and democratic society.

Fundamental Freedoms

2. Everyone has the following fundamental freedoms:
   (a) freedom of conscience and religion;
   (b) freedom of thought, belief, opinion and expression, including freedom of the press and other media of communication;
   (c) freedom of peaceful assembly; and
   (d) freedom of association.

Democratic Rights

3. Every citizen of Canada has the right to vote in an election of members of the House of Commons or of a legislative assembly and to be qualified for membership therein.

4. (1) No House of Commons and no legislative assembly shall continue for longer than five years from the date fixed for the return of the writs at a general election of its members.

(2) In time of real or apprehended war, invasion or insurrection, a House of Commons may be continued by Parliament and a legislative assembly may be continued by the legislature beyond five years if such continuation is not opposed by the votes of more than one-third of the members of the House of Commons or the legislative assembly, as the case may be.

5. There shall be a sitting of Parliament and of each legislature at least once every twelve months.

Mobility Rights

6. (1) Every citizen of Canada has the right to enter, remain in and leave Canada.

(2) Every citizen of Canada and every person who has the status of a permanent resident of Canada has the right

(a) to move to and take up residence in any province; and

(b) to pursue the gaining of a livelihood in any province.

(3) The rights specified in subsection (2) are subject to

(a) any laws or practices of general application in force in a province other than those that discriminate among persons primarily on the basis of province of present or previous residence; and

(b) any laws providing for reasonable residency requirements as a qualification for the receipt of publicly provided social services.

(4) Subsections (2) and (3) do not preclude any law, program or activity that has as its object the amelioration in a province of conditions of individuals in that province who are socially or economically disadvantaged if the rate of employment in that province is below the rate of employment in Canada.

Legal Rights

7. Everyone has the right to life, liberty and security of the person and the right not to be deprived thereof except in accordance with the principles of fundamental justice.

8. Everyone has the right to be secure against unreasonable search or seizure.

9. Everyone has the right not to be arbitrarily detained or imprisoned.

10. Everyone has the right on arrest or detention

(a) to be informed promptly of the reasons therefor;

(b) to retain and instruct counsel without delay and to be informed of that right; and

(c) to have the validity of the detention determined by way of habeas corpus and to be released if the detention is not lawful.

11. Any person charged with an offence has the right

(a) to be informed without unreasonable delay of the specific offence;

(b) to be tried within a reasonable time;

(c) not to be compelled to be a witness in proceedings against that person in respect of the offence;

(d) to be presumed innocent until proven guilty according to law in a fair and public hearing by an independent and impartial tribunal;

(e) not to be denied reasonable bail without just cause;

(f) except in the case of an offence under military law tried before a military tribunal, to the benefit of trial by jury where the maximum punishment for the offence is imprisonment for five years or a more severe punishment;

(g) not to be found guilty on account of any act or omission unless, at the time of the act or omission, it constituted an offence under Canadian or international law or was criminal according to the general principles of law recognized by the community of nations;

(h) if finally acquitted of the offence, not to be tried for it again and, if finally found guilty and punished for the offence, not to be tried or punished for it again; and

(i) if found guilty of the offence and if the punishment for the offence has been varied between the time of commission and the time of sentencing, to the benefit of the lesser punishment.

12. Everyone has the right not to be subjected to any cruel and unusual treatment or punishment.

13. A witness who testifies in any proceedings has the right not to have any incriminating evidence so given used to incriminate that witness in any other proceedings, except in a prosecution for perjury or for the giving of contradictory evidence.

14. A party or witness in any proceedings who does not understand or speak the language in which the proceedings are conducted or who is deaf has the right to the assistance of an interpreter.

Equality Rights

15. (1) Every individual is equal before and under the law and has the right to the equal protection and equal benefit of the law without discrimination and, in particular, without discrimination based on race, national or ethnic origin, colour, religion, sex, age or mental or physical disability.

(2) Subsection (1) does not preclude any law, program or activity that has as its object the amelioration of conditions of disadvantaged individuals or groups including those that are disadvantaged because of race, national or ethnic origin, colour, religion, sex, age or mental or physical disability.

Official Languages of Canada

16. (1) English and French are the official languages of Canada and have equality of status and equal rights and privileges as to their use in all institutions of the Parliament and government of Canada.

(2) English and French are the official languages of New Brunswick and have equality of status and equal rights and privileges as to their use in all institutions of the legislature and government of New Brunswick.

(3) Nothing in the Charter limits the authority of Parliament or a legislature to advance the equality of status or use of English and French.

17. (1) Everyone has the right to use English or French in any debates and other proceedings of Parliament.

(2) Everyone has the right to use English or French in any debates and other proceedings of the legislature of New Brunswick.

18. (1) The statutes, records and journals of Parliament shall be printed and published in English and French and both language versions are equally authoritative.

(2) The statutes, records and journals of the legislature of New Brunswick shall be printed and published in English and French and both language versions are equally authoritative.

19. (1) Either English or French may be used by any person in, or in any pleading in or process issuing from, any court established by Parliament.

(2) Either English or French may be used by any person in, or in any pleading in or process issuing from, any court of New Brunswick.

20. (1) Any member of the public in Canada has the right to communicate with, and to receive available services from, any head or central office of an institution of the Parliament or government of Canada in English or French, and has the same right with respect to any other office of any such institution where

(a) there is a significant demand for communications with and services from that office in such language; or

(b) due to the nature of the office, it is reasonable that communications with and services from that office be available in both English and French.

(2) Any member of the public in New Brunswick has the right to communicate with, and to receive available services from, any office of an institution of the legislature or government of New Brunswick in English or French.

21. Nothing in sections 16 to 20 abrogates or derogates from any right, privilege or obligation with respect to the English and French languages, or either of them, that exists or is continued by virtue of any other provision of the Constitution of Canada.

22. Nothing in section 16 to 20 abrogates or derogates from any legal or customary right or privilege acquired or enjoyed either before or after the coming into force of this Charter with respect to any language that is not English or French.

Minority Language Educational Rights

23. (1) Citizens of Canada

(a) whose first language learned and still understood is that of the English or French linguistic minority population of the province in which they reside, or

(b) who have received their primary school instruction in Canada in English or French and reside in a province where the language in which they received that instruction is the language of the English or French linguistic minority population of the province,

have the right to have their children receive primary and secondary school instruction in that language in that province.

(2) Citizens of Canada of whom any child has received or is receiving primary or secondary school instruction in English or French in

Canada, have the right to have all their children receive primary and secondary school instruction in the same language.

(3) The right of citizens of Canada under subsections (1) and (2) to have their children receive primary and secondary school instruction in the language of the English or French linguistic minority population of a province

(a) applies wherever in the province the number of children of citizens who have such a right is sufficient to warrant the provision to them out of public funds of minority language instruction; and

(b) includes, where the number of those children so warrants, the right to have them receive that instruction in minority language educational facilities provided out of public funds.

Enforcement

24. (1) Anyone whose rights or freedoms, as guaranteed by this Charter, have been infringed or denied may apply to a court of competent jurisdiction to obtain such remedy as the court considers appropriate and just in the circumstances.

(2) Where, in proceedings under subsection (1), a court concludes that evidence was obtained in a manner that infringed or denied any rights or freedoms guaranteed by this Charter, the evidence shall be excluded if it is established that, having regard to all the circumstances, the admission of it in the proceedings would bring the administration of justice into disrepute.

General

25. The guarantee in this Charter of certain rights and freedoms shall not be construed so as to abrogate or derogate from any aboriginal, treaty or other rights or freedoms that pertain to the aboriginal peoples of Canada including

(a) any rights or freedoms that have been recognized by the Royal Proclamation of October 7, 1763; and

(b) any rights or freedoms that may be acquired by the aboriginal peoples of Canada by way of land claims settlement.

26. The guarantee in this Charter of certain rights and freedoms shall not be construed as denying the existence of any other rights or freedoms that exist in Canada.

27. This Charter shall be interpreted in a manner consistent with the preservation and enhancement of the multicultural heritage of Canadians.

28. Notwithstanding anything in this Charter, the rights and freedoms referred to in it are guaranteed equally to male and female persons.

29. Nothing in this Charter abrogates or derogates from any rights or privileges guaranteed by or under the Constitution of Canada in respect of denominational, separate or dissentient schools.

30. A reference in this Charter to a province or to the legislative assembly or legislature of a province shall be deemed to include a reference

to the Yukon Territory and the Northwest Territories, or to the appropriate legislative authority thereof, as the case may be.

31. Nothing in this Charter extends the legislative powers of any body or authority.

Application of Charter

32. (1) This Charter applies

(a) to the Parliament and government of Canada in respect of all matters within the authority of Parliament including all matters relating to the Yukon Territory and Northwest Territories; and

(b) to the legislature and government of each province in respect of all matters within the authority of the legislature of each province.

(2) Notwithstanding subsection (1), section 15 shall not have effect until three years after this section comes into force.

33. (1) Parliament or the legislature of a province may expressly declare in an Act of Parliament or of the legislature, as the case may be, that the Act or a provision thereof shall operate notwithstanding a provision included in section 2 or sections 7 to 15 of this Charter.

(2) An Act or a provision of an Act in respect of which a declaration made under this section is in effect shall have such operation as it would have but for the provision of this Charter referred to in the declaration.

(3) A declaration made under subsection (1) shall cease to have effect five years after it comes into force or on such earlier date as may be specified in the declaration.

(4) Parliament or a legislature of a province may re-enact a declaration made under subsection (1).

(5) Subsection (3) applies in respect of a re-enactment made under subsection (4).

Citation

34. This Part may be cited as the Canadian Charter of Rights and Freedoms.

Glossary of Terms

aboriginal self-government   greater autonomy of First Nations to pursue their own political, social, cultural, and economic objectives with limited interference from the federal government

administrative law   body of legislation that details the rules civil servants must follow in doing their jobs

administrative-coordinative department   department that facilitates the operation of government services

amending formula   a legal process for changing the constitution

attorney general function   the function of the federal Department of Justice to safeguard the legal interests of the federal government

authority   government's ability to make decisions that are binding on its citizens

bicameral legislature   a government structure that consists of two Houses of Parliament; in Canada, the House of Commons and the Senate

bill   a proposed law

bureaucracy   the organizational structure through which government exercises its power

bureaucrat   public servant

bureaucratic entrepreneur   a model of public policy in which bureaucratic experts within government come up with policy ideas and then approach elected officials to obtain the resources and public legitimacy necessary to implement their programs

bylaw   a local or municipal law.

Cabinet   the government body that consists of MPs appointed by the prime minister who oversee government departments and act as advisers in major policy areas

Cabinet solidarity   the united front that Cabinet presents on given policy matters, although individual Cabinet ministers may privately be opposed

capitalism   an economic system based on private ownership and competition in a free market

charismatic authority   authority based on the unique talents and popular appeal of an individual

Charter of Rights and Freedoms part of the Canadian constitution that guarantees certain fundamental rights and freedoms to all Canadians

civil service people who are directly tied to the administrative function of a particular level of government

classical technocratic a model of public policy in which decisions originate with politicians, who then provide bureaucrats with clear direction as to what should be done

common law a body of law that has grown out of past court cases and is based on precedent or custom

community policing approach to policing based on the police and the community working together

Confederation the union of former British colonies that resulted in the formation of Canada on July 1, 1867

constituency department department that provides services directly to citizens

constitution a document that outlines the basic principles of government of a country and the fundamental rights and freedoms enjoyed by its citizens

continuity the long-term or ongoing nature of a bureaucracy

cost sharing funding of provincial programs that combines federal contributions with provincial funding

delegated legislation legislation handed down from a parent department that grants a regulatory agency political powers

department government division responsible for carrying out some aspect of government policy

deregulation reducing or eliminating bureaucratic processes that may hinder private enterprise and limit economic growth

discretionary power interpretive flexibility granted to some government employees to act within a given setting

division of powers jurisdiction over major policy areas, as divided between the federal and the provincial governments

economic efficiency ability of a business to maximize profit and minimize expense

executive branch (federal) the branch of government that includes the monarch's representative (governor general), the elected head of state (prime minister), and Cabinet

executive branch (provincial) the branch of government that includes the monarch's representative (lieutenant governor), the elected head of state (premier), and Cabinet

expertise   knowledge of or ability in a particular area or subject

federal spending power   the power of the federal government to raise the greatest share of tax revenues

federal system   Canada's government structure, which divides political power between the federal government and the provincial governments, with greater power resting in the federal government

government   a formal system within which political power is exercised

government bill   a bill proposed by a member of Cabinet

hierarchy   an organized system of labour characterized by a superior–subordinate relationship

human relations   management approach that recognizes and addresses the personal and social needs of individuals

impersonality   the objective nature of jobs and routines in a bureaucracy, based on written rules and records

isolationism   an economic remedy characterized by refusing to trade with other countries

judicial branch   the branch of government that consists of the court system

jurisdiction   sphere of influence or power

laissez-faire capitalism   free-market capitalism (French for "leave alone")

left-wing   a political attitude or philosophy that favours more government intervention to help achieve social equality

legal authority   authority based on the rule of law

legislative branch (federal)   the lawmaking branch of government (House of Commons and Senate)

legislative branch (provincial)   the lawmaking branch of government (Legislative/National Assembly)

legislative union   a structure of government in which power is concentrated in a central Parliament

legitimacy   the moral obligation citizens feel to obey the laws and pronouncements issued by those in authority

majority government   a government that includes more than half of the total MPs in the House of Commons (in 2000, this required 151 MPs of a total of 301)

member of Parliament   an elected representative in the House of Commons who represents a riding

minimalist state   approach to government in which state resources are used in the interest of the business, or capitalist, classes, to promote individual wealth and economic growth

minister of justice function the function of the federal Department of Justice to monitor federal legislation, directives, and regulations and to consider other justice-related issues

ministerial responsibility principle of parliamentary government that makes ministers responsible for the official activities of their departments

minority government a government that has the greatest number of MPs in the House of Commons but not more than half of the total MPs

multiculturalism cultural and racial diversity; in Canada, a constitutionally enshrined policy that recognizes the diversity of our population

municipal council the governing body of a municipal government

neoconservatism a conservative political philosophy that argues that government should revert to the limited role it played at the beginning of the century, particularly in social and economic areas

new public management an approach based on the belief that government has overextended itself by doing too much and becoming preoccupied with bureaucratic procedure

party loyalty the requirement that all members of a political party vote according to the wishes of their leader

patriation the process of removing the Canadian constitution from British control and bringing it under Canadian control

police services board civilian board that oversees a local police service

policy-coordinative department department that coordinates policy across government

policy instrument method employed by governments to ensure compliance with public policy and to achieve their goals

political culture the basic attitudes people have toward each other, the state, and authority

political spectrum a model that shows political philosophy on a continuum from left to right wing

politics the social system that decides who has power and how it is to be used in governing the society's affairs

politics–administrative dichotomy theoretical framework that views politics as the decision-making apparatus of government and administration as performing the implementation function

portfolio department

private bill a bill proposed by a senator

private member's bill a bill proposed by a non-Cabinet MP

protectionism   an economic remedy characterized by protecting domestic products with tariffs, import quotas, and other barriers to trade with other countries

public administration   the branch of the political structure, consisting of public employees, that turns the policy decisions of elected politicians into action

public good   the complex of publicly funded goods and services that contributes to the collective well-being of a state

public policy   what government does or does not do

public service   the civil service

representative government   government that is based on members elected by citizens to represent their interests

responsible government   government that is responsible to the wishes of its citizens, as embodied in their elected representatives

right-wing   a political attitude or philosophy that favours more individual freedom and less government intervention

rule of law   the concept that all citizens, regardless of social rank, are subject to the laws, courts, and other legal institutions of the nation

scientific management   management approach based on using resources in ways that maximize productivity and minimize waste

stagflation   a situation where an economy experiences high unemployment and high inflation at the same time

subjudicial rule   rule that prohibits government officials from commenting on an issue that is before the courts

theory of representativeness   theory that if the public service is to be responsive to the needs of all Canadians, it should represent a cross-section of Canadian society

traditional authority   authority based on heredity, religion, or divine right

triple E Senate   a Senate that is equal, elected, and effective